KEPT
BY THE
POWER

KEPT BY THE POWER

GLENYS LEWIS

HAZARD PRESS
publishers

CONTENTS

FOREWORD

The buzz of lively conversation in the ballroom suddenly died as an official walked to the front of the guests. Clearly and calmly, as one accustomed to ceremonial occasions, he outlined what was to follow – a vice-regal investiture in Government House, Wellington. It was Thursday, October 28, 1993.

Among those whose services were to be recognised was Glenys Lewis, priest of the Anglican Church in New Zealand, to be awarded the honour of Commander of the British Empire (CBE) the accepted abbreviation for its longer, original title: Ordinary Commander of the Most Excellent Order of the British Empire.

The nominees sat in reserved places until their turn came to receive the recognition to be bestowed by Her Excellency, Dame Catherine Tizard, on the Queen's behalf.

In an adjoining drawing room, Glenys waited with three others – a knight, a dame and another to be granted the CBE – to receive the highest awards. Eventually they were escorted into the ballroom to join the others.

A hush fell over the gathering and all stood as the Governor-General entered. Members of her staff were at her side as she addressed the assembled guests.

Glenys walked up to the dais as her name was called, a tall, elegant woman of eighty-two, still not quite believing what was happening to her that day. An official read the statement outlining her remarkable achievements and Glenys received the warm congratulations of Dame Catherine as she pinned on the medal.

Amid well-deserved applause, Glenys returned to her chair, her CBE the only one awarded to a priest in the Anglican Church worldwide in the Queen's

Glenys at her investiture with Governor-General Dame Catherine Tizard.

Birthday Honours of 1993.

Glenys has had an eventful life. Born in Wales in 1911, she experienced joy and pain in childhood, enduring friendships and unusually sad separations, and success in training for several careers in adulthood.

As a committed Christian, Glenys has believed all her life that she is 'kept by the Power.' Her unwavering faith in her Lord, coupled with her own inner strength, her determination to pursue her vocation and her lively sense of humour, has won the admiration of her friends and colleagues – though not always on their first encounter with this woman of spirit and courage.

Wary of the challenge she often presented and unsure how to deal with her, many of those in authority in hospitals, schools and churches could not at first believe what they were hearing from Glenys. But while disconcerted to find their authoritarian manner questioned by a woman who didn't take kindly to being bullied, most of them were sooner or later won over by Glenys's charm and humour and became her good friends.

This is her story, in which Glenys speaks for herself, something she was always able to do, even as a child – and that is where her story begins.

– Aline Pengelly

PREFACE

When I was in my teens we used to sing a chorus:

> Kept by the Power of God
> Kept by the Power of God
> Day by day
> Come what may
> Kept by the Power of God

These words have been a direct experience throughout my life. When I began to think and discuss about writing my memoirs with a friend, she suggested that I write about some of my experiences of being 'kept by the Power of God' and have that as the title. She suggested this because today many people are unable to relate to the words God, Jesus, or Christ. Yet many people are aware, some only subconsciously, of a power, a spiritual power, outside yet within, beyond yet present. To some of these people God, Jesus and Christ, are known only as swear words, or associated with Christmas and Easter: times of holidays, eating too much, and receiving presents.

Some people would put my experiences in this book down to chance, coincidence, luck. If so, I have been very lucky. On the other hand it is possible to consciously link oneself to a power greater than human, a cosmic power. A power of love. And then to hand over one's life to be guided, used and protected by that same power. By so doing, chance, luck and coincidence have no place in one's life.

So I believe. And therefore in the preface I will state with deep conviction my belief in a personal saviour Jesus Christ, Son of the Living God, that He has been a faithful companion throughout the years – not remote, high in the sky, but ever present, a living reality within me. My wish is to share this with you.

CHAPTER ONE

Childhood: Memories of Love and Loss

I just lay there in that great double bed with its deep feather mattress that I seemed to be sinking into. I felt so lost and so very lonely. As I lay there in the spare bedroom of my Aunt Dege's house I tried to understand what had happened to me. I was seven years old and a few hours earlier Daddy had come to the house to see me. We were in the sitting room and I was on his knee with his arms around me when he told me that I wouldn't see Mummy again, that she had 'gone to be with Jesus.' He held me tight as he told me this, trying to comfort me and console me. His loving gesture was to affect me emotionally for many years.

It seemed to me that only a few days earlier I had been with Mummy. I had been told I was going to stay with Aunt Dege in Cardiff, to me a long way from Penarth where I lived. Mummy was in bed because she was ill, so I went to her bedroom to say goodbye to her. As I left her and went towards the door, suddenly I turned and ran back to the bed, jumped on it, threw my arms around her and said, 'Mummy, I *do* love you so much.' Now here I was, alone in the spare room in Aunty Dege's house, wanting to be with Mummy in Penarth where I would be safe and happy again. I couldn't cry… I just felt lost.

For the first seven years of my life I had been surrounded by love and care, so it was not surprising that I was unprepared for the death of my mother which was to shatter my security and change my life. I did not realise the full effect of this tragedy until fifty years later, when I was living in Auckland. One night I had a vivid dream that I have never forgotten.

I was a little girl in a little boat coasting down a river. I felt quite happy and secure, even though I was alone and had no paddles, because I knew that Mummy and Daddy were in a boat behind me. Suddenly my little boat started to toss and turn as it met another river going in the opposite direction. I was very frightened. Suddenly Daddy appeared, not from behind me, but from the far side of the other river. He took me in his arms and saved me. Even so, I was still terrified.

Penarth was a seaside town not far from Cardiff, in Wales. I lived there with Daddy, Mummy, Enid (three years older than me) and Gwenda, a baby I hardly knew. Maggie was the cook and Nanny looked after us. I was three years old when World War I broke out so I knew little about it. We did not suffer directly as a family, as two uncles survived army service, and Dad was in a reserved occupation as he was an agricultural merchant serving a large area.

We never lacked food – the farmers Dad dealt with saw to that. Butter was rationed, and I can still see a large butter dish for the four of us and a smaller one each for Maggie and Nanny. Dad was very strict where food was concerned and I remember once refusing to eat my rice pudding. After a long battle of wills with Dad I was allowed to get down from the table and went off to bed very happy at winning the battle. Imagine my horror when I found a plate of cold rice pudding at my place next morning instead of the lovely breakfast that everyone else enjoyed. I had to eat it, and eat it I did!

Our house was three-storied and on the third floor Dad had a billiard room where he would play with his friends. Enid was about nine and I was about six when Dad had small billiard cues made for us and taught us the basics of the game. Little did he know that forty years later I would be entertaining a doctor in an isolation hospital in Bombay with a daily game of billiards!

Enid and young Glenys with their beloved mother.

In the garden we had a swing and how I loved going high and fast, especially standing on the seat. At the bottom of the garden we kept chickens, and bantams for Enid and me. We had to look after them and their eggs were especially for us. There was a croquet lawn, and again Dad had mallets made for Enid and me so that we could learn to play. Mummy and Daddy had parties of friends in to play, but I do not recall that we were allowed to play with them. I imagine not. Again, little did Dad know then that more than sixty years later, in another country, I would start to play croquet again. What a great dad I had!

Enid and I spent most of our time in the nursery, where Nanny reigned supreme. This was where we played and fought, as all kids do. It was a large room with a fireplace and a high guard in front of it, a piano to practise on, a clotheshorse with a pulley to take it up to the ceiling out of the way, and a very large rocking horse.

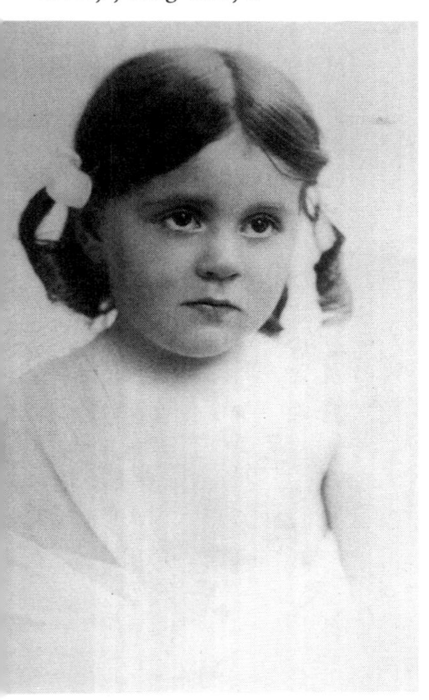

A very young Glenys.

Enid and I slept in a room at the top of the house, next door to the bedroom the maids shared. In those days nobody thought it odd that these two women were expected to share a bedroom, despite the disparity in their ages. They had no privacy or place that they could call their own. This was the norm in the first decade of this century, however strange and unacceptable it seems to us now in the last.

In our bedroom we had a window looking out towards the sea. Enid used to love to tease me, and one night persuaded me that the Germans were coming and would climb through our window. I was scared stiff. If Mummy was going out to dinner she would come up to see us in that room, looking lovely and smelling delicious. She would sing for us, 'Jesus, tender shepherd, hear us, bless thy little ones this night,' then give us a kiss and a hug. How we loved her.

We were also allowed in the drawing room

occasionally and I remember playing once with Enid and a boy whose name I have forgotten. Enid and the boy were going to get married and I had to marry them. (Foretaste of things to come!) After the 'service' they went behind the sofa for their honeymoon.

We were taught to swim at an early age – I would have been about five. We went to an indoor swimming pool, in those days called 'the baths,' and the teacher would put a kind of harness over my shoulders and lower me into the water, I would scream madly and hate it. But I soon learned to love it and since then swimming has been one of my great joys, especially in the sea, doing battle with the waves.

Enid had a bicycle and when Nanny took us out I would badger Enid to let me have a go. On I got, with Enid holding on behind me, and I felt quite safe until suddenly I realised she *wasn't* holding on – and I immediately fell off. I have always been very grateful that we were given the chance to learn these things when we were so young.

Family portrait.

We always had a cat and a dog in our home. The cats seemed to live in the kitchen area but the dogs were part of the family. I have met many people since who do not like cats and are afraid of dogs, and I think this is mostly because they were not brought up with them in the home.

One time Mummy and I went on holiday to Weston-super-Mare, the other side of the Bristol Channel. It must have been when Mummy was in her last illness. I had been taken out of school to go with her as I had been very ill as a baby and was considered frail and in need of plenty of fresh air. Mummy befriended a woman staying at the same place who had a son about my age, so we played together. One day we went alone up on the sandhills, and David told me that he would marry me when we were grown up. I liked that idea. His mother later sent me a photo of David standing by a sundial and I hung it above my bed for years, but I never saw David again.

It was soon after that holiday that Mummy died of tuberculosis.

From that night my memory is a complete blank until I find myself in a seaside town called Porthcawl: in a different house, with the same maids – Maggie and Nanny, Mummy's sister, Aunty Shan and Daddy. My most vivid recollection of that time is of one day when Enid, Gwenda and I were upstairs in the nursery, and Daddy and Aunty came into the room to tell us they were going to be married. Enid and I jumped all over them; we were so happy because we loved them both. We went to their wedding dressed to the nines, with flowers around the brims of our straw hats.

For a few years we were very happy. We lived by the sea, which we all loved passionately. Frequently in the summer we would walk miles over the downs to Rest Bay, with our bathing gear and picnic things and our dog Rap rushing ahead of us. We would find a niche in the rocks, spread our things around

Enid and Glenys prawning with Dad at Horton, Gower Coast, Wales.

and set Rap to guard our corner and keep intruders away. Bathing was our great joy. I remember one day when the sea was rough and no-one was bathing. Daddy took Enid and me in and we had a lovely time fighting the waves. It was made especially good as we had a crowd of spectators; it made me feel very brave! The rocks on the beach were a great challenge to us and we would play follow-the-leader, daring each other to take risks as we leapt great chasms, or so they seemed to us.

Often I would take Gwenda out in the pram, and one day I accidentally tipped her out and she started to cry. I was most alarmed until I found she was only crying because she thought she had dirtied her fur bonnet! I was very relieved.

We had a garage at the bottom of the garden with an upstairs to it. The large rocking horse that had been in the nursery at Penarth was put into this room as our present nursery was not big enough. The fun we had up there with our friends and our imagination running full rein was great.

As a family we went to the Baptist church every Sunday, where the minister was the Reverend Arthur Davies. He was to become a great friend of Dad's and we loved him. Later I was to nickname him 'Do-ray-me.' The first Sunday of each month was a children's service and Mr Davies would tell us stories out of the Bible in place of a sermon. We were set the task of writing about it afterwards. We had to have a nome de plume so I called myself Florence Nightingale. Each month the best story would earn a prize. I won one or two and valued them very much.

But, alas, these halcyon days were to end. It would have been about 1920 when Enid was home from boarding school for the summer holidays and became ill. I can remember her sitting on the potty on the floor of her bedroom unable to get up. A doctor wrongly diagnosed rheumatic fever and she was therefore given the wrong treatment.

As the days passed Daddy got more and more worried. In the end he took her to Cardiff to see an orthopaedic specialist, who diagnosed poliomyelitis. That began years of pain for Enid, who had to wear irons on her legs and ghastly jackets to strengthen her spine. I was too young to appreciate what she was going through but it must have been terrible for her as she had been a real tomboy, into all activity and mad on swimming as I was. The specialist in Cardiff told Daddy that if he had left it another week before taking Enid to him, she would never have walked again. But Enid not only survived, she went on to live a normal life.

About this time we were to have another sister. I knew nothing about it until one day I was told not to go into the spare room, and to stay at school for lunch. Of course I did go into the spare room, only to find a pram. I was disappointed not to find something exciting. But when I came home later that day there was my new baby sister, Jean. I do not recall asking any questions; we didn't in those days, and we were not put 'in the picture' at all. Strange, when one thinks of the awareness and knowledge that youngsters have these days.

More sadness was to follow. Jean's Mummy, our stepmother, was not well. One day I was in the drawing room with Daddy and he called me over. When he tried to take me on his knee I fought him like a wild-cat. Subconsciously I must have linked this with the time he told me Mummy had died. I was afraid it was going to happen again. Gwenda was too young to be aware of what was going on, but Enid and I were aware of a great sadness in the house and knew that something was wrong with this Mummy too.

About a year after Jean was born we left Porthcawl and went to live in Cardiff. We had a lovely home there overlooking a park and lake. It was a square house called The Knoll, with five bedrooms and a tennis court in the garden, but alas, it did not help Jean's Mummy get better. Probably Daddy had known this would be the case, but wanted us to be closer to our relatives, most of whom were in Cardiff.

It was difficult for Enid and me to leave Porthcawl and our friends: we had been so happy there, and we loved the sea so much. With all this sadness in our lives and moving from place to place it is a wonder Enid and I did not become insecure little girls. Possibly we would have if Dad had not been such a rock in our lives.

At the time of the move to Cardiff, in about 1922, Enid would have been about fourteen years, I came next at eleven years, and Gwenda was four, Jean's Mummy died, also of tuberculosis, just before Christmas 1924.

The memorial service was held at Aunty Dege's, so that the women could be present. It was not 'done' in those days for women to attend at the graveside. I don't know why the service was not held in a church. I do know that there were no crematoriums in those days with chapels provided.

Enid and I were there and everybody was crying. I was in trouble within myself because I couldn't cry. I felt that was quite dreadful of me, so I tried very hard. I wanted to cry – I was feeling very sad inside – but no tears would come.

This inability to cry has dogged me all my life and seems to get more difficult as I get older. Looking back over my 87 years I can see quite clearly what a profound effect the death of my mother had on my emotional development. To cry is almost impossible for me. I envy my friends when they go to the cinema or watch TV and weep into their hankies! Even when I am moved all that happens is that I may get a lump in my throat. I regret this, as a good cry can be a wonderful release of emotions.

It seems also that my father holding me on his knee with his arms around me to tell me of the death of my mother had a lasting effect on my ability to form attachments to men. Although I have been attracted to men, I have never married. It seems there has been a block in me that has made it almost impossible for me to give myself wholly. Always there seems to be a part of me that withholds and is a 'looker-on'.

The days following must have been very difficult for Daddy. Here he was with a fairly large house and four girls too young to take over the running of it. Maggie and Nanny had coped marvellously as a temporary arrangement while Jean's Mummy was ill, but early in 1925 a housekeeper arrived.

I remember her as a short, elderly woman who never made any impression on me. She would take Enid and me to town and buy us the most expensive clothes. Of course we loved it and were happy to be spoiled in this way. But she appeared to think that Dad was made of money and after about six months he had to ask her to go.

During her time with us I was given a pretty free hand, which was nice at the age of twelve or thirteen. In the park across from our house was a large lake with three islands in it. A part of this was for swimming and the rest was for rowing boats, which were for hire.

Over the summer my friend Valerie and I spent most of our free time from school either swimming in or rowing on the lake. We loved it. Valerie had a boyfriend called Norm, and I had a boyfriend called Ken, and they would join us. One time we cycled to Wild Park, just beyond the big park, and across to a shelter. Valerie and Norm went into one partition and Ken and I went into another, and Valerie told me afterwards that she and Norm kissed! No such luck with Ken and me. By today's standards our relationships were incredibly innocent: we thought it very daring even to kiss.

One day I was at the park gates with three boys and our bicycles. Valerie had gone to her house for something. To my instinctive horror, I saw my Aunt Addaline, Dad's sister, walking towards me. Somehow I knew that she would not approve of me being at the park gates with three boys, and I was right. I said to the boys, 'Crumbs, for goodness sake, hide me!' But of course they couldn't. My aunt did not even slow her pace, she just walked past me with her nose in the air, and commanded in passing, 'Glenys, come with me!'

The four sisters in 1924. From left: Gwenda, Enid, Glenys and Jean. Glenys's new bike was a reward for passing a music exam.

I knew I was in deep trouble as I was called 'Glen' in those days and 'Glenys' only if I was in disgrace. Even though I knew instinctively that she didn't approve of what I was doing, I had no idea why.

Not a word was spoken as we went home, but a week later Aunt Addaline called to take Enid and me in the car with her daughter Dilys. Apparently I was still in the dog box as I was put to sit with Lane, the chauffeur, in front of the glass partition. I felt very bewildered and unhappy.

What she had told Dad I do not know – nothing was ever said. But what I do know is that I was sent to boarding school a few months later. The effect of this on me was quite traumatic. What was wrong with talking to boys in the open in broad daylight? Shouldn't they have been glad that I was friends with some of the male sex since we were all girls in my family? Even our first cousins were all girls. I was completely ignorant about the physical differences between male and female: that was never discussed. Dad had his dressing room and never once did I see him without some clothing on.

Intercourse? I had never heard of it. Where did babies come from? I did not have a clue. I was left with this strange feeling that what had happened at the park gates was wrong, almost unclean, but I did not know why.

That incident would have happened about June. It was our family custom for Dad to take the whole month of August off so we would go to the seaside for a month. This particular year he had no-one to accompany him and somehow it transpired that a Miss Shepton came to join us when we went to Bude in Cornwall for our holiday that year. She was young, maybe in her late twenties; very attractive and full of fun. We liked her – then – and it was a wonderful holiday.

In those days families did not stay in caravan parks or motels. The normal thing was to stay in a guest house, or boarding house, I think they were called. Usually one or two other families would be staying in the same place and we would eat together at a long table. The other family with us on that holiday was a doctor's wife and her son and daughter, and we did things together. We went for walks when it rained and sang loudly along the country lanes, or played on the beach and went in the sea. The doctor's wife had a two-seater car and one day Alec, the son, and I were playing in the car and Alec pushed me into the dickie seat (the back of the little car, which could be used as a boot or a seat). As he was pretending to shut me in, his mother came out and went for me. 'Don't play with my son like that! Don't cheapen yourself!' She was really angry. Once again I was made to feel guilty about being in the presence of a boy, and still I had no idea why.

After the month was over and we came home, Miss Shepton came with us and became our housekeeper. The master bedroom was a lovely room opening onto a verandah and she occupied that while Dad moved into his dressing room. I think we could have coped with that all right, but we hated her for wearing our Mummy's clothes, even to her furs. I can recall one dress in particular. It was a navy blue georgette with rosettes in pale blue ribbon all over it. I must have loved that dress to be able to see it so vividly still today. However, one thing Dad did not let her have was the jewellery from his two wives, which we were to inherit later in life.

Although Enid and I had no awareness of any 'goings on', obviously Maggie and Nanny could not cope and they left, to our great sadness. We loved these two, who had been family to us for so long.

CHAPTER TWO

Boarding School and Beyond

I was sheltered from much of the unpleasantness at home in those first months after Miss Shepton's arrival as a few weeks after our return from Bude I went off to boarding school. This was in Arley Castle, near Bewdley, Worcestershire.

The building had a portcullis, courtyard and a tower with a winding stone staircase. At the top was a flagstaff where the Girl Guides had to splice the flag at dawn and bring it down at sunset. Halfway up the tower was a classroom and we would run up and down those winding stone stairs as if we were running on the flat! I have vivid recollections of that room. We were fourth-formers and pretty naughty. Our poor form mistress had no idea how to keep order, though she was a brilliant academic.

Arley Castle.

I remember sitting on the wide stone windowsill with a drawing pad and trying to draw the wonderful scene I could see of rolling green country and lovely trees. The castle grounds were fantastic. There was a walled garden in which we played tennis; an arboretum – a park of beautiful trees; a Naboth's Vineyard, so called for the collection of trees and shrubs from all over the world. The latter was out of bounds, which made it especially interesting, and we would run through there to get to the village – also of course out of bounds. Each morning before breakfast we had to run around the arboretum, rain or shine, winter or summer. We became expert at knowing the short cuts!

We avidly read novels by Angela Brazil, with their stories of fabulous midnight feasts and exciting adventures at boarding school, and we at Arley Castle did our best to live up to those tales. Parents would send us 'tuck', which somehow we would secrete under the floorboards of our dormitory, and we would sneak up bread from a meal. The appointed night would arrive and we would take it in turns to keep watch and then wake the next one until it was midnight. Then we would start our feast. We only had our tooth mugs so everything had to go into them, whether it was sardines or fruit salad. We ate with great relish, feeling very daring as we did so. Funnily enough, next morning we would go down to breakfast ravenous and ready to eat a hearty breakfast.

Teenagers can be cruel. One night we visited another dormitory after lights out, just for the fun of it. The matron walked in and said, 'I will not have these nautical visits,' to which we all with one voice said, 'You mean *nocturnal* visits, Matron!' How humiliating for her.

Four Arley girls: Glenys, Dee, Sidda, Hermoine, Connie.

One winter term we were to have a fancy-dress ball. By this time we were calling Miss Shepton 'Aunty.' I was full of excitement for this ball and asked during the holidays, 'Aunty, could I please have a fancy dress to take back for next term?'

'No,' she said. 'I am not going to spend money on that. If you want one, make one for yourself.'

After much thought I asked Aunty Dege if she had an old-fashioned nightie she could lend me, and she had. Then I bought some pink ribbon and threaded it through the lace at the neck and cuffs and bought a baby's dummy. The night of the ball arrived and we all dressed in our outfits. I felt a bit ashamed of mine as some of the costumes were very grand indeed. During the parade I shuffled along, baby-walking and sucking my dummy, in Aunty Dege's nightie. When I was asked who I was I replied, 'Princess Elizabeth.' At that time our queen was just a baby, and I won first prize for initiative and simplicity of outfit!

Those of us who were strong swimmers were allowed to swim in the River Severn, just below the castle grounds. We had to cross on the tiny ferry boat to come from the station. The river was comparatively small, but it could be treacherous with its potholes and irregular surface.

One day the Guide captain, on whom I had a schoolgirl crush, and one or two of the other teachers took the Guide pack for a picnic along the riverside. We came to a spot where the leaders thought it would be safe for all of us to bathe, even those who could not swim, as it was not deep right across. We all rushed in with much noise and rejoicing. We swimmers had just found a good swimming spot when suddenly we saw someone splashing with her arms in the air. At first we thought she was playing, as she was so close to the bank, but no, she was in real distress. I shall never forget the feeling when I realised I would be the first to reach her. I had heard how a drowning person could grab hold of her rescuer and drag her down, and I was frightened and for a second wanted to slow down. However, that feeling didn't last long and I got to the panic-stricken girl as she was going under for the third time. The other swimmers caught up with me and we brought her to shore. Afterwards we would joke that she had been in greater danger of drowning while she was being rescued, despite our lessons in lifesaving!

On the occasion of my eightieth birthday, she wrote in a letter:

Glenys was a tall, lovely, active, popular girl, good at sports and art but already showing a reflective side. She was always great fun and a splendid companion. I have reason to know she was a good swimmer as I shouldn't be here today if she hadn't towed me out of a fast-flowing River Severn during a Guide picnic.

She was alive and that was all that mattered. That day a special bond was formed that has held for sixty-five years. To this day Vera and I keep in touch, even though she is in England and I am in New Zealand.

I really loved my days at Arley Castle, although academically I did not do very well. Before Arley I was forever being taken out of school to benefit from 'fresh air' and my schoolwork suffered badly. I was forever trying to catch up and never succeeding, so in the end I didn't bother trying; I just enjoyed myself. Even so, I managed to pass the Senior Oxford Examination.

I was home from boarding school for the May holidays, three months before my seventeenth birthday. I had one more term to go before leaving school. Daddy had arranged to take Enid and me to a ball and we felt very grown up and very excited.

The great day came and we made ourselves as attractive as possible and clung to Dad with great expectation and trepidation. As it turned out I found myself thoroughly enjoying the evening, chiefly because one particular man took a lot of interest in me and kept asking me for dances. Although he was years older than me, towards the end of the evening he asked, 'Could I phone you and arrange to take you out one evening next week?'

Glenys aged about seventeen.

'I'm sorry, but I go back to boarding school in a few days for my last term,' I replied.

'Well, in that case, I will have to leave it for now, but I will phone you in August.'

The family teased me quite a bit about this: we called him the Count. But that was that, or so I thought.

Not so. One day in August he duly phoned me and asked if I would come out with him to tea and the cinema. You will notice that he had changed the time from evening to afternoon. Initially I must have given him the impression of being older than I was! I agreed to go with him and we fixed a date and time. Afterwards I thought, 'What will Dad say, me arranging to go out without asking him first?' To my surprise and relief he didn't seem to mind.

The day came and I met him outside the café next

door to the cinema. We sat at a table for two. I must have been talking animatedly as I knocked over a plate of cakes full of cream and they splashed onto the floor. I went on talking as though nothing had happened! 'The Count' must have been full of laughter within, but he never blinked an eye, just motioned to the waitress to replace the plate as we carried on our conversation.

He took me home as far as the entrance to our driveway. I did not ask him in. We chatted there for a bit and he asked me if I would go out with him again the following week. I said yes.

When I went inside Dad asked, 'Well, did you enjoy yourself, and did you like him?'

'Yes, I did enjoy it and the Count was all right and I am going out with him next week… okay?' To which Dad replied 'Yes' and left it at that.

The following week the procedure was the same except that I did not knock over a plate of cakes. But I did not enjoy myself so much – he was telling me things about his life that I didn't like the sound of. We were Baptists and Sunday was a day that was special and apart. But he told me that he went to his club on Sundays to play billiards! I was not amused – I must have been a proper little prude.

About halfway through the pictures I urgently needed to go to the loo, and I didn't know how to cope. I pretended I didn't like the picture and the Count asked if I would like to leave, to which I replied that I thought so, and didn't he as well? So we got up and left. However, I let myself down badly when we got to the foyer, because I did not know where to find the loo and had to ask him. He took me home as before and asked me out again, but this time I told him I could not manage next week. He said he would phone me, but he never did. I don't really blame him.

Once again when I got home Dad asked me had I enjoyed myself. This time I replied, 'No, I didn't. I don't like him very much, and I am not going out with him again.'

Dad amazed me by saying, 'I am not surprised. He is a very worldly man and old enough to be your father. I did not think you would like him.'

I gasped. 'Dad! Yet you let me go out with him! Why?'

'If I had said no to you, you would have wanted to go out with him all the more, and you would have made something special of him. Whereas, if I just let you go out with him, I knew I could trust you to find out for yourself what he was like.'

I have never forgotten this very sound advice.

About the same time there was another example of my father's wisdom in dealing with a teenage daughter. A school friend and I wanted to 'try our wings.' She lived in the Midlands in England and came to stay with me at my home in Cardiff. From there we went to stay in a posh hotel in Bournemouth in the south of England – alone! It still amazes me that our parents allowed us to go. But Dad was pretty cunning. He said that he and Aunty (my stepmother) would go and stay in Bournemouth while I was there. 'That's okay, so long as you don't stay anywhere near Noggy and me,' said I.

I never found out where they stayed. Noggy and I went by train and took a taxi to this fabulous hotel that had a ballroom and an indoor swimming pool. Noggy and I could imagine ourselves dancing with tall, good-looking men, and racing the same men in the swimming pool. How great was our disillusionment! The hotel had all the fabulous things we had expected, but... the *men...* where were they? Our fellow guests were all elderly, to us – *old* married couples – and there was *no* dancing. Clearly we had to find our excitement outside the hotel, so the next evening we set forth. Eventually we found a place where there was wining, dining and dancing. We had dined, so we sat at a small table at the bar and tried to look as though we did this every day. Neither of us knew what to order. I remember quite distinctly that I had Crème de Menthe. I have never liked it since! After a little time three young men asked if they could join us and we spent the evening with them.

When it was time to go home they asked us if they could give us a lift, and we said yes. Where was home? they wanted to know, and we gave them the name of the hotel. They had two cars so the one who had been with me said he would take me in his car and the other two could take Noggy. Neither of us was in the least nervous or unsure. But after a short while I noticed that my driver was not going the right way, and before I could say anything, there we were down on the beach. Then he started to put his hand on my leg, and I threw it off and said, 'Oh no you don't! Take me to the hotel at once!'

'Don't tell me you are *really* staying at that hotel!' he said, and without more ado he reversed the car and took me there, where Noggy was waiting with the two young men looking very worried. They asked if they could take us out the next night and we both said no. They said they would call for us anyway, and the next evening we watched them arrive and eventually leave when we did not appear. We went to the pictures. All our lovely dreams…

After that holiday Dad said to me one day, 'Can you remember what you were doing that Saturday night about 10pm? I had a strong feeling that you were in danger of some sort, and I prayed for you.' I believe it was his prayers that protected me that night. I wish I had shared that experience with him and told him how grateful I was. I wish I had told him what his prayers meant to me, and the love and respect I felt for him for the trust he put in me.

I left school just before my seventeenth birthday in August 1928. Dad asked me what I wanted to do and I said that I didn't have the remotest idea. So he arranged for me to go to Cardiff Technical College for a year, where I learnt shorthand, typewriting and book keeping. It was a good year of no responsibility and plenty of fun. At the end of the year, just as Dad had paid the fee for me to sit my finals, it was announced to the students that there was a clerical vacancy at Powell Duffryn, one of South Wales's coal exporting firms. The offices were down in the docks, which were very busy in 1929. Two of us applied and I didn't think I had much chance of winning the job as the other girl's shorthand was much faster, but to my surprise I was offered the job and asked to begin the following Monday, the day exams were to start.

Whatever will Dad say? I thought as I prepared myself to tell him. Surely he would be mad with me for throwing away the chance of certificates when he had paid the entrance fee and all. But he wasn't angry, in fact he said, 'I think the experience of working with a prestigious firm like Powell Duffryn will be of more value than any certificate.' What a father.

I spent a year there and never even touched a typewriter, nor did I do any shorthand. Despite that, I was given two rises in one year. Not bad, I thought. To start with I was nothing more than an office boy. My first day there I had to work late because the manager, Mr Dutton, hadn't finished his correspondence and I had to see to it and post it. I was staying with an aunt at the time and when I arrived home late and in tears, my aunt and uncle were angry.

'Never mind, Glen, you won't need to go back there tomorrow. I'll phone Mr Dutton in the morning,' said my uncle.

'No you won't,' said I between my tears. 'I shall be going back in the morning.' And I did. By now I was showing definite signs of 'stickability.' I like that word: one who doesn't easily give up; one who is prepared to stick at it when things are tough.

While I was working down at the docks I lived at home and went to the Baptist chapel every Sunday with Dad and the family. Dad had been brought up Church of England, along with his brother and sister, but it had meant very little to any of them. Their mother was Church of England and their father a Baptist. As a young man Dad had been quite a man-about-town, popular with the ladies, and when he was in his early thirties he was close to being engaged to a society lady. At the time his brother was dying of 'creeping paralysis', as it was called then, and could not speak. Yet one day he asked Dad to read him a passage out of the Bible. Dad was to see this as a miracle and it turned his life upside down. He also fell in love with Mary Davies, the nurse who was caring for his brother, and they married, and both joined the Baptist Church. She of course was my mother.

As a child I loved Jesus and He was very real to me. During my years at boarding school that awareness got pushed out. The Church of England was the local church, and there we would have to go Sunday by Sunday. The vicar we thought very old... and oh, so dull! We sat as far back as we could and did not behave very well.

When I left school and once again started to go to chapel every Sunday, I was also pretty bored. One day my sister Enid announced that she was going to be prepared for baptism and I said, 'If you are going, I might as well go at the same time.' Enid was horrified. 'You don't go forward for baptism in that casual fashion! Whatever are you thinking of? You have to believe in and love Jesus before baptism. That's why it's called Believer's Baptism.' One Sunday after the service I waited in the corridor while Enid went in to talk to the parson, Mr Hagger. A strange thing happened to me while I waited in that dim, narrow corridor – I started to weep and I was still weeping when I went in to see Mr Hagger. It became obvious that I had experienced a real conversion and had recaptured my awareness of the reality of Jesus Christ. When the day came for us to be totally immersed during baptism, coming out I had no feeling of being wet, only of great joy.

This conversion produced in me a desire to serve God in some way, and I felt it had to be in a full-time capacity. At that time the obvious outlet was the missionary field and I thought I would like to be a nurse in China. But the various people I told all said the same thing. It was wonderful that I had a desire to serve God, but I must leave it to God to decide whether or not it would be in China. They were all thinking of my bad health record; not one of them could see any missionary society looking twice at me. I still have two of their letters and as this is a record of my life I include them here.

3 January 1929
'Morlan'
Blundell Avenue
Porthcawl

My dear Glenys
I am deeply grateful to you for your sweet and beautiful letter. Of all the many Christmas and New Year greetings which I received your inspiring letter with its noble message was the most precious.

Let me congratulate you from the bottom of my heart upon the step you have taken. It is the greatest decision you have ever made and the greatest-but-one which you can ever make. But you will ask what then can be greater? It is this! That you will decide to become submissive to the Will of God. I am glad to note in your letter that you have not forgotten this.

What I mean is this. Circumstances may arise which will prevent you ever entering upon service in any foreign field. What then? Even so, you will not cease to be a missionary. It is the spirit of a person which makes him or her a missionary and not their sphere of labour…
Your most sincere friend and well-wisher,

Arthur Davies

20 November 1928
'The Fron'
Newton, Mont.

My dear Glenys,
I think it is very good of you to let me have the good news and I want to thank
you, dear, for letting me share your happiness.

Of course I am not surprised, but when you say it is 'wonderful' you use
exactly the right word. And I hope that life will continue to be full of 'wonder'
for you as the years go by.

You have now deliberately, of your own free decision, entered upon a life
of highest service. Ever since I have known you I have known your heart to
be full of love, and of the faith which dwells with love; but now this faith and
this love have brought forth the fruit of a great decision.

Now dear, as to the 'form' that service is to take: you have confided to me
what you think. And what I want to say is this: If you are willing, and if God
is willing, then you may be perfectly sure that the way will open which is to
lead you to that vocation. But if it doesn't, then you must not get a sense of
disappointment and failure. For if the way doesn't open, it simply means that
you are being called to some other kind of service. The great thing is the
willingness to serve, and that willingness must include the leaving of the form
of service to God.

The longer I live the more sure I am that there is a Providence which
shepherds our lives. And this itself is one of the 'wonderful' things of our faith.

I can see that you are very happy. I want you to be happy always. But (it
seems a strange thing to say) don't depend too much upon happiness itself,
for that would mean that you would be making even your 'religious' self the
centre of your interest, and that would be most unhappy in the long run...

You are living in a 'wonderful' world, and the years – the long years – which
I trust are before you will see many 'wonderful' happenings. There is a great
work to be done, and you are one of the workers. Christ's Kingdom is coming
– and that is the most wonderful thing of all.
God bless you,
Ever your friend

Gwilym O. Griffith

These two wonderful friends, who loved me through their deep friendship with my father, and who knew our family and my health history well, were preparing me for the inevitable. At the time I was, of course, thrilled to get such lovely letters, but with the optimism of youth I went ahead with my plans to be a medical missionary in China.

Dad was dead against my training to be a nurse. He never told me why, but as I look back I can understand his reasons. In those days nursing was really hard work: a thirteen-hour day with two hours off in that; lectures, study, assignments; and ward work which included day-to-day care of the patients but also sweeping, cleaning, dusting and being a waitress. Dad knew how tough it was because my mother had trained at the very hospital, Cardiff Royal Infirmary, that I was applying to. I think he in part blamed that heavy work for her death from TB. Also, because I was delicate he dreaded I would myself develop TB. Then there was the small matter that I couldn't stand the sight of pain or blood. I had only to see someone in pain for everything to go black before me. Funnily enough, at the time none of these factors seemed to dent my enthusiasm to go nursing.

Dad knew Sister Gibbs, in charge of a men's medical ward, and he arranged with her that she would talk to me and do her best to 'put me off'. While I was waiting to see her I had to stand outside the ward waiting. As I stood there and saw all those men lying in their 'beds of pain' sure enough everything started to go black and then I heard the voice of Sister Gibbs saying, 'Hey! Girl! Whatever is the matter with you? Come into my sitting room at once.' She applied the necessary treatment and then proceeded to tell me what I was letting myself in for if I carried on with this ridiculous idea. 'Look at you, you can't even stand looking at patients, let alone nursing them! Whatever makes you think you could be a nurse?'

But it seems nothing would put me off. I was going to be a medical missionary in China. To my delight the matron accepted me for training.

My next step was to give in my notice to Mr Dutton. When I told him of my plans he said, 'Why in the world do you want to go to China? Do you want to be eaten by lions?' We laughed and I assured him that there were no lions in China as far as I knew. I was sorry to leave as he had been a good boss and I had enjoyed working for him.

CHAPTER THREE

Nursing Training

The first thing to hit us as we entered the Preliminary School for nurses was our pride. We were twelve in our intake, and we had been provided with a uniform; dress, apron, cap, belt and cuffs. The hem dress was about thirteen inches from the ground and we were all horrified and felt very dowdy, but we thought we had no alternative but to wear them.

Starting nursing training.

The Prelim School was in a separate house from the hospital, and we had to go back there for our meals. All the nurses had their meals in the very large dining hall. Our first visit there left us with our mouths agape. Not one nurse was wearing her uniform as long as ours! We were delighted and all spent our first evening shortening our dresses. We soon realised how fortunate we were, as we were told that the intake before ours had had to wear long hair in a bun at the back of the head. We were saved from this as the senior surgeon had a daughter in that intake, and it was through him that this archaic rule was abandoned.

For our first two months it was purely theory we studied, plus some first aid, such as bandaging. We stayed up all hours or arose very early, all of us very anxious to pass our entry examinations on anatomy, physiology and the like.

We all did pass, and the great day came when we were each allocated to a ward. I was sent to Llanbradach Ward, a women's surgical ward. Everyone said the sister there was a real tartar and woe betide anyone who got on the wrong side of her. I thought I was doing well until one morning I went into the sluice room, to clean it and tidy it ready for Sister's round (inspection) when she came on duty. I found a lot of water on the floor and there didn't seem anything there with which to wipe it up. So I went to the staff nurse and asked her what I should do.

'Oh, don't bother me, just use some of the soiled linen to wipe it up,' she replied.

I must say that I thought this very odd, but of course I did as I was told. Sister started her round and when she came to the cleaned sluice room she spotted one very dirty pillowcase. She went straight to the staff nurse and said, 'Which nurse is responsible for cleaning the sluice room in the side ward?'

The staff nurse told her, and Sister told her to fetch me to her room.

'Nurse, I understand that you cleaned the sluice room where I found this pillowcase. Will you please tell me what you were doing with it?'

When I told her I thought she would burst, she was so angry.

'What kind of a home have you been dragged up in that you use pillow-cases to wipe up dirty floors?'

I couldn't let that pass, so I told her I had been told to use the soiled linen. That put me properly in the apple-cart, because of course she wanted to know who had told me to.

'I don't remember.'

She would not take that and kept on and on until I was nearly in tears.

'Very well, if you won't tell me you go straight down to Matron with the pillowcase in your hand.'

It is impossible to describe the awesome fear we had of Matron, so I was shaking in my shoes when I said, 'I won't tell you!'

Dead silence as Sister stared into my eyes. Then suddenly her face broke into a lovely smile and she said, 'That's good, nurse, I'm so glad you didn't tell me. I like a nurse who is loyal to her colleagues.'

After that incident she was very good to me. Little did I know then that eight years later I was to be a patient in her ward for many months, where I would receive nothing but kindness from her.

The junior 'pro' (probationer), 'mucky pro' as we called ourselves, was responsible for one side of a long ward. This would entail giving out bedpans, washing the bedridden; making beds with another nurse, pulling the beds out from the walls to sweep the floor under them, dusting and tidying the lockers, and caring for 'your' patients' needs.

About my second day I was taking the bedpans in and out one at a time when one of the patients said, 'Nurse, dear, they usually bring in three or four at a time; if you don't you will be all behind.' As the patients were in for at least week, most of them two to three weeks, we did get quite fond of them, and they of us. They would refer to you as 'my nurse' and it gave you a nice warm feeling, especially when they asked if 'my nurse' could take them to the operating theatre. One reason was that they saw a lot of us because we worked thirteen-hour shifts. There were only two shifts in twenty-four hours: the day shift and the night shift. The day shift was on duty at 7am and off at 8pm, with two hours off each day. We had an evening and a day off each week, so we would finish at 6pm, say, on a Friday and have to be back in hospital by 10pm Saturday evening. And woe betide anyone who was late – they would be locked out of the nurses' quarters, and would be on the mat the next day.

After only a week I was told that I would be taking my first patient to the operating theatre, and that I was to spend the morning there, as one after another patients came up for surgery. I felt very important as I took up the first patient, who was to have her appendix removed. It was a very simple operation, but I had to stand beside the anaesthetist and be ready to do anything he wanted. (It was rare indeed to see a woman anaesthetist; my sister Gwenda was one of the pioneers, about ten years later.)

Although I was excited about going to theatre I was also of course apprehensive. How would I cope with the sight of blood, or of anyone in pain? I would also react badly to the smell of ether or chloroform. However, I stood there and as the operation began I kept on saying to myself, 'Glenys, this is very interesting, very interesting, very interesting…' All the time the theatre was disappearing and everything went black. I had been told that if you fainted in theatre they just pushed you under the table! I didn't want that, so with my arms stretched out before me I made my way to where I thought the door should be. Someone caught up with me and guided me to a chair beside the window in the ante-room. When I felt better I went back inside, but I didn't last long and out I had to go again. When the operation was over the theatre sister rang the ward, spoke to the sister and asked for another nurse. 'The one I have here is more trouble than the patient!'

You can imagine how I felt. I was sent off duty and I went to my room, a ghastly cubicle without a window, with wallpaper peeling down from the ceiling, and wept. I though I was finished as a nurse.

But the body is amazing; determination and stickability even more so. When I was sent back to the same operating theatre ten days later with a patient who had two hours' surgery, I never turned a hair – not then or since.

While still a junior nurse I was working in the Ear, Nose and Throat Department, which consisted of a ward and an outpatients' clinic. The sister was in charge of both. The outpatients' clinic was served by three specialists in ENT, and they would see the patients together in a large room, half of which was screened off for the waiting patients to sit, so it was easy for them to hear what was going on on the other side of the screen. One morning Mr Prichard, one of the ENT surgeons, shouted to the sister, 'That speculum is no good, I have thrown it on the floor in that corner. Fetch it, re-sterilise it and bring it back to me.'

Sister said never a word but went to the corner, picked up the speculum and did what she was told. I was astounded and horrified, and vowed to myself, 'If anyone treats me like that, I will refuse to pick it up and he can whistle for it.' And I meant it, although my resolve was not put to the test until my third year.

The years passed and I became a staff nurse. We were given a considerable amount of responsibility and authority, but as we had yet to take our finals we were still in training. I was made staff nurse of the ENT Department while

Sister was on her annual holiday and I was delighted. The day came for out-patients, and the three surgeons had a steady stream of patients waiting behind the screen. Suddenly a voice bawled out, 'Staff Nurse, I have thrown the speculum into the corner; fetch it, sterilise it and return it to me.' No please or thank you. My words of three years ago rang in my ears: here was my test. Were they empty words?

With my knees knocking, I turned to Mr Prichard and said, 'The speculum will stay where you have thrown it for the rest of the morning.' Deadly silence while we each glared into the eyes of the other. The patients behind the screens must have been entranced as they would have heard every word – and probably my knees knocking!

Suddenly his face broke into a wide grin. 'Okay nurse, you win, and the speculum stays in the corner for the rest of the morning.' We got on well after that, and he always treated me with respect. It also taught me a lesson. Never, but never, give in to a bully. That lesson has stood me in good stead many times; there are plenty of bullies around, of both sexes.

The assistant matron, Miss Henderson, was a short rotund figure, to us pretty old, with a waspish tongue. We called her 'Tot.' Frequently she would be on duty in the large dining hall, to make sure we behaved ourselves. One night while we were still in the Prelim School, the meal was tripe, which I have never been able to cope with. I left mine on my plate, and Willis, next door to me, left some bread on hers. As we trooped out at the end of the meal, Tot commanded Willis and me, in front of all these wonderful nurses, to stay behind.

She sent us back to our seats, me to eat my tripe and Willis her bread. Out of the side of my mouth I said, 'Willis, I'll eat your bread if you eat my tripe.' So we did a hasty swap, right under her beady eye, and thought we'd got away with it. But when we got up to go she ordered us to stay where we were until every nurse had left the hall. They all filed past our table and we felt such fools. When there were only the two of us left she gave us such a dressing down. What kind of homes had we been dragged up in? I had heard that before and my hackles rose. I had to say that there was nothing wrong with my home, thank you very much. But she ranted on and then left us to go down the stairs while she used the lift. Willis started to howl with laughter and I said, 'Keep it up, she will think you are crying!'

Lectures and study took place out of our 'free time' and Miss Henderson had the job of correcting our written work. One day I knocked and waited for her to say 'enter', which she did, and then she proceeded to scold me in her Scottish burr, 'Nur-rse, Nurrse, do you have to disturb me just to bring your written work? For goodness sake, Nur-rse, don't knock, put it on the chair by the door and go away.' The next time I had to give in work, I stood outside her door wondering what to do. Eventually I took the bull by the horns and entered without knocking.

'Nur-rse, Nur-rse! Where were you brought up that you think you can enter a private room without first knocking?' Here she was again attacking my home. I told her what she had told me to do.

'Oh, go away, Nur-rse. Don't be such a nuisance, and shut the door after you…' Poor Tot. She would not be able to talk to nurses in training like that these days, but this was sixty years ago.

It was in my second year that I noticed that my profuse sputum began to be bloodstained. I felt I should report it but I was reluctant to do so, fearing the worst. In the end I filled a test-tube with the sputum and took it to Sister Gibbs, the sister in charge of the men's medical ward, where I had nearly fainted before I started to train. She was aghast when she saw it and I remember saying to her, 'I think it is bronchiectasis.'

'Girl! Don't be so stupid. Only old men who are heavy smokers get that!' So she ordered me down to the home sister straight away, who showed an equal amount of horror and immediately I was put to bed in a women's medical ward. I was taken straight out onto the balcony for fresh air, because before any tests were even taken they had diagnosed tuberculosis. It was not really surprising, as my mother and her sister had both died of that disease, but strangely enough, I had never even considered it a possibility – the symptoms didn't seem right to me.

Test after test was taken of my sputum, but they could never get a positive result, much to my delight. They were mystified! Eventually I was taken out of the ward and sent home to rest for some months, with the result that I was in my fourth year when I eventually took my finals.

The one superb thing that came out of that delay was that when I returned, I joined another intake and in that intake was Enid Llewellyn Williams. We became wonderful friends, and this friendship carried on long after our training was over, until her tragic death in her early fifties.

We shared a room when we were senior nurses: it was a great treat to be in a two-bed room. It was at that time that she met her husband-to-be, when her father took her on a cruise and she and the ship's doctor fell in love. She eventually married Dr Emyr Wyn-Jones, and they went to Liverpool where Emyr became a much-loved heart physician. I will come back to Enid later in my story.

My days off were precious and my usual practice was to go home to The Knoll. I would be in bed by 10pm and sleep the clock round until 10am, hardly moving throughout the night, so tired I would be. Enid three years my senior, had also been through the Cardiff Technical College and was now working too, so I did not see as much of her as I did of Gwenda and Jean. Gwenda would have been about twelve and Jean about nine when I started nursing, and they were avid in their desire to hear any gory or exciting detail of my life at the hospital. Dad couldn't stand it, and always told us to find somewhere else to talk. I loved talking about my work, and they must have loved it too, because Gwenda was to become a doctor and Jean a nurse!

During these years my church-going had to take a back seat as our hours were so irregular. But my faith kept strong, along with my desire to serve, although my health told me that missionary work was not to be.

For my finals, we had to go to Swansea for the oral and practical tests. I was very nervous as I was so anxious to pass. The first matron to examine me was kind and gentle, which was just as well because I found myself incapable of speech! It is a fact that in fear or terror, one's mouth can go so dry that it is impossible to get a word out. The matron said very kindly, 'Nurse, try to pull yourself together as the next matron you will see will not be understanding and you must be able to answer her questions.'

Wasn't that kind of her? It helped me to overcome my nerves sufficiently so that I passed all my oral and practical tests. For many years after that experience, if I was at all nervous my mouth would go very dry.

Some time later we came off night duty to find the place humming. The results were through. Once your envelope was in your hand you knew whether you had passed or failed even before opening it: if the envelope was thin you had passed; if it was bulky you had failed. My envelope was thin!

I left hospital about 8.30am to go home and the streets were full of people going to work. I could not make out why everyone who passed me stared at me, and I began to think I had a smut on my nose. Suddenly I realised I was walking along with a broad grin on my face. I was very happy. I had passed in my loved profession and now I was a state-registered nurse – how absolutely wonderful!

CHAPTER FOUR

From Midwife to Matron

Later in 1934 I began midwifery training at Bristol General Hospital. Dad thought it would be good for me to complete my qualifications by becoming a state-certified midwife. But if I had done this in my original training school it would have taken twelve months and included a lot of heavy lifting and carrying as the building was very old fashioned. Dad did not think my health could cope with this so he paid a considerable sum for me to train in another hospital as a student sister, with no menial work involved and only a six months course. This was how I came to do my further training in Bristol. We worked very hard, but as senior nurses, our work was solely to do with the patients and our studies.

My first visit to the labour ward remains with me still. It was an abnormal birth, and I thought what a dreadful process this giving birth must be. Later, when I had seen plenty of normal deliveries, I was to be enthralled at the wonder of the human body. Left to itself the body would know exactly what to do as the baby's head rotated until it was in the right position to emerge. It was important to supervise this rotation and often one had to use all one's strength to hold back the head until it was fully rotated, otherwise it would come out too quickly and the perineum would tear and have to be stitched. In the days when I trained, this was considered a disgrace and a bad delivery.

Today, I am told, the perineum is deliberately cut and then stitched after birth. This shocks me. Unless it was an abnormal birth, the midwives did the delivery, whether in hospital or in the home, and we would never have dreamed of cutting the perineum during labour. Why and when did this policy start? Was it when doctors took over deliveries in hospitals, and home deliveries became a thing of the past? It is good to know that here in New Zealand there is a move to bring the midwife back as the one to deliver the baby.

One or other of the student sisters had to be on call at night in case of emergencies, and we were given three minutes to be up, dressed in full uniform – cap, belt, cuffs, apron, the lot – and downstairs.

One night I was called, met the doctor and off we went through the night to a house where a woman was haemorrhaging. Fortunately we were able to save her and all was well. The next day I was working in outpatients with a patient who was behind screens. Two doctors came in, the doctor of the night before and a student doctor. The doctor said to the student, 'You see Sister here? Well, look at her well, note her hair, nothing out of place. She looked like this at 3am and I had timed her from when she was called and it took three minutes. How could she do it, I ask you? Those two rolls under her cap were as they are now, and all her uniform neat and tidy. Incredible! Tell us, Sister, how do you do it?'

'Quite easy, I wear a wig!'

He looked at me for a split second, not sure whether I was serious or not, then he saw the twinkle in my eye and we all had a good laugh! This ability to dress in haste has stood me in good stead many times since.

The work we did in the district I found quite fascinating. People who could not pay for midwifery services were dealt with from the hospital. This meant that we were dealing with poor people, and very loving and grateful we found them. Often the call would come at night and the midwife who responded would take along a student such as myself. We would go by taxi. On arrival we would ask for plenty of hot water and newspapers. The woman in labour would often have been scrubbing the floors a few hours before – actually one of the best things she could have been doing. I doubt if we would have had much support for that theory from the upper grade, where mostly the women were cosseted and not allowed to move a finger: quite the worst treatment. It didn't surprise us that the women we served usually had easy and normal births.

For eight days after the birth we would visit the mother and child daily, on our bicycles, bathing the baby, attending to the mother, and giving the necessary advice if it was her first child. She would be soon up and about her work.

I loved the six months: the work in the wards, the delivery room and the district. The whole experience taught me so much. The miraculous wonder of our bodies and of new life; the amazing fortitude of a woman in labour, who would say over and over again, 'I'll never go through this again' and yet, once the baby was in her arms, could say, 'It was worth it.'

Only once in my future life did I use my midwifery knowledge, but I was never to forget the many lessons I was taught. One of those was my need to grow in 'stickability' as, once again, my plans and my training had been disrupted by my health. I had had another haemorrhage and been admitted to hospital again.

Fortunately this time I was put into the hands of a physician who suspected that I had bronchiectasis! He told me a drug had been discovered, called Lipiodol, which could be inserted into the bronchials and would show up on an X-ray if there was any abnormality. He asked if I was willing. Of course I was willing.

The house physician, the sister, and the radiologist duly arrived in my room with a portable X-ray for the event. The liquid was put down my larynx and, not surprisingly, I began to choke – apparently I went blue and lost consciousness. When I came to, I found the sister leaning over me in tears, saying, 'I will never let this be done to you again, you poor dear!'

Apparently, all had not gone according to plan. When the specialist found out what had happened he was very angry with himself and said, 'I am so very sorry to have put you through this. I should have done it myself or made sure the houseman knew exactly what to do. He failed to anaesthetise your larynx, so naturally it would object to fluid going into your lungs.' In the next five years I was to have that X-ray a further three times. The anaesthetic had to be injected through my neck and it was a most distressing exercise.

However, the result showed that I did indeed have bronchiectasis. The lungs have air passages going through them like the veins in a leaf, and this condition means that the walls of the air passages break down and form cavities. These in turn fill up with sputum, which has to be got rid of by coughing.

The specialist told me that there was nothing to be done for this condition, and that it was bad luck that mine seemed to be of the bleeding type. All he could suggest was not to work too hard. He sent me to the seaside to a convalescent home, and said he had arranged with the matron for me to have my own room.

I went down by ambulance with another woman, who spent the whole journey talking about her ailments. When we arrived the matron said 'I am very sorry but we have no single rooms, so I have put a four-bed room at your disposal. I am afraid I will have to put one other with you. Would you like the woman who travelled down from Bristol with you, or would you like another woman who is coming from Birmingham today?' Spare me! Without hesitation I replied, 'Preserve me from the woman I travelled with. I will take the woman from Birmingham!' I was not in the room when she arrived, but she told me later that she was scared stiff that I would be a 'holy-roller' because I had a Bible on my locker! That first evening we found a room with a fire in it that was unoccupied, and we sat there together in the quiet. We discovered that we both read the same kinds of book and liked the same things, and found that we both had a sense of humour. I have happy recollections of those two weeks, chiefly of Bud and I hanging on to the promenade rails in gales of laughter. Thus began one of my greatest friendships which spanned about fifty-six years until she died.

After those two weeks away I returned to hospital determined to finish my training. To my dismay, however, my specialist told me that when I had finished my midwifery training I would have to give up hospital nursing and suggested I should try taking a job as a matron in a boys' preparatory school. He found me a temporary matron's position for one term at Clifton College in Bristol and I found I loved it. I found I had no difficulty with discipline, so I could enjoy the boys and have fun with them.

At the end of the term I heard of an English hospital at Cannes on the French Riviera that wanted nursing sisters for private work. This I thought would be fun, so I applied. After an interview with the matron in London I was accepted for the season, from late November to mid-March, the time when the wealthy fled the colder climes and went to the Riviera. When I got to Cannes I was told that the matron normally only took nurses who had trained in London at either Guy's, Bart's or St Thomas's hospitals, so I considered this a feather in my cap. I had not told the matron of my complaint as it was quiescent at the time and I did not expect it to erupt again, especially when my job was to be so light.

To test myself out as a private nursing sister before I went I did six months' private nursing around Cardiff, and was pleased when all went well. I was very nervous about travelling to Cannes on my own, never having been overseas before. At the Gare du Nord in Paris the porter thought I had under-tipped him, which no doubt in my ignorance I had. So he gathered his chums and they stood at my door shouting abuse at me in French. Just as well my French is poor! I kept my head down and pretended they weren't there. I was glad when the train started to move out of the station.

I loved Cannes, and I loved the work. I was sent to a large hotel in Grasse, the heart of French perfume country, where a colonel and his wife had gone down with grippe – the 'flu. He was in the big bedroom and she was next door with a communicating door. He warned me sotto voce that his wife was a bit of a tartar but said not to be frightened of her. Then one day I took his temperature and he asked what it was. 'I never tell my patients their temperature,' I said.

'Oh, don't you, Sister?' he bawled. 'But you *will* tell me! If you don't I will read it myself.'

'Oh no you won't. The thermometer goes out with me.' We glared at each other and then he smiled. He realised who was the boss in the situation and we got on marvellously after that, although no-one else would go near him. The waiters asked me even to take him the menu to spare them being barked at! His wife was actually a dear.

A young Danish man about twenty-four was staying at the hotel and we got friendly. He asked me to go to the cinema with him. I asked the colonel's wife for time off and when she found out why she sent for the maitre d'hôtel to ask if the young man was a suitable consort for 'her' sister! The cinema was a village hall with a sheet hung in one corner and we saw the picture on that. We thoroughly enjoyed our evening and we remained friends until he saw me off on the train from Cannes, travelling as an invalid myself, with a sister in tow. Afterwards he sent me pictures of Denmark and his home, but that was all, which was just as well as my emotions were not involved at all.

My last assignment was to St Tropez to nurse an Englishman who was ill. But my own body was to let me down badly. One night I had quite a severe haemorrhage from my lung and was forced to notify the hospital and return to Cannes. I was put into a single room and treated as if I had rampaging tuberculosis. Everything that came into my room had to be fumigated and my eating utensils kept separate. No amount of assurance from me would make them change that practice. They were sure I had TB and that was that. What they wrote to my father I never found out, and what it cost him to get me home I do not know.

The matron arranged with my father that I should return to London and go straight to the Brompton Chest Hospital for diagnosis and treatment. I travelled as an invalid, being lifted on and off the train and the ship to Dover. How I hated that! But the sister who travelled with me was a bad sailor so she went below and left me on deck, much to my relief. I was reclining on a chaise longue when a tall, very handsome man came up to me and asked if he could sit down by me. He arranged for tea to be served and we had a very pleasant time chatting together. He was Portuguese and very distinguished. As we approached Dover he said, 'Would you do me the honour of dining with me tonight at my hotel?'

I had to reply, 'I would really love to, but unfortunately I have another engagement.' He accepted that very graciously. I did not tell him that my engagement was with the Brompton Chest Hospital! I was thankful that he was one of the first to leave the ship at Dover as I could not have borne it for him to see me carried off on a chair.

My sister Enid had come from Wales to meet the ship and she took me straight to the hospital. Within twenty-four hours my own diagnosis of bronchiectasis was confirmed. What a relief that was. I knew I was right but the way I had been treated had made me doubt myself.

I stayed at the hospital for a couple of weeks, having what little treatment they could give me. I also had an operation – on my nose! It was a partial ethmoidectomy, or removal of a bone in the upper part of the nose. It was

The new matron at Gadebridge Park.

an extremely painful, unpleasant operation and I suffered from terrible headaches for some time. However, life had to go on, and I returned to Wales, where for about six months I did nothing but be at home and visit friends.

When I was better I applied for and was appointed to the position of matron of Gadebridge Park, a boys' preparatory school in Hemel Hempstead, one of the home counties around London. The beautiful old manor house was set in large parklands with a small river, the Gade, winding through the grounds. There was a bridge over the river and I vividly remember one night returning from London about 11pm, walking through the park only to find the bridge occupied by cows. I had always been terrified of cows and I didn't know what to do. I stood there cow-gazing for a time and then said to myself, 'Come on, girl, you can't stand here all night. Don't be a coward.' So step by step I elbowed my way over the bridge and through the herd, and I am still alive!

I started work at Gadebridge Park in September 1936, at just twenty-five years of age, which in those days was very young for such a responsible position. I loved it, but it was not to last.

CHAPTER FIVE

My Tiresome Body

Things were going along very happily at Gadebridge Park when out of the blue, my bubble burst. It was a Sunday morning and I was walking back from church when suddenly I had a severe haemorrhage from my lung. When it was over I walked on back to school. From my experience in Cannes I knew it was better not to tell anyone, especially the headmaster. They would all have a fit, and in their ignorance assume mortal danger to their pupils from TB. So, after lunch I let it be known that I didn't feel too well and said I would rest in my room for the afternoon.

However, I knew I couldn't leave it at that. I wrote to Dr Ewing, the specialist who had looked after me at the Bristol General, and asked him what he thought I should do. He wrote back a warm and understanding letter that contained some surprising news. Apparently, since I had left Bristol, a new kind of surgery had been carried out in Europe and in Wales to operate on lungs to remove lobes – lobectomy. He also told me that a surgeon at the Cardiff Royal Infirmary was having considerable success. His name was Mr D'Abreu, and Dr Ewing suggested I go and see him.

I couldn't believe it! Mr D'Abreu was a surgeon with whom I had worked when I was in training! I knew him. I liked him. I had every confidence in him. This was wonderful. But it meant I had to leave my beloved school, which I did at the end of my fourth term, December 1937, and I like to think that everyone was sad to see me go. I still have in my possession a treasured reference from the headmaster, Mr Lindsay.

In 1938 I made an appointment with Mr D'Abreu, and we greeted each other like old friends. However, to my surprise he was cagey about his work, telling me the mortality rate was still very high. He said I was to go away for three months to think it over, and if I decided to go ahead he would see me again. He also said the decision was to be mine. He would not advise me; neither were my parents to give me advice.

At the end of three months I went back to him and told him I wanted the operation. I had decided it was worth the risk. My illness hung over me all the time, and that threat was preventing me from getting on with my life. Anyway, if it was not a success, I would not know much about it!

It was about eighteen months later that Mr D'Abreu told me that on the morning he was to operate on me, he lay in his bath and thought, 'I cannot do this operation. It is bad enough taking such a risk with someone I know only through consultation – but I know Glenys. I like and admire her and her courage. How can I operate on her?' Thinking back on this now, I realise that it must have been much more difficult for him than it was for me. It is hard to believe today that doctors can perform heart transplants and so on. Back then there were no blood transfusions, no antibiotics if things went wrong.

I took the preparation very calmly. I was just so glad that at last something was going to be done. I remember taking out a library subscription as I knew I would have a long time in hospital and convalescing. I could see myself reading book after book. How wrong I was!

It must have been about August when I went into the Cardiff Royal Infirmary and was admitted to Llanbradach Ward. The same sister was still in charge, so you can imagine how I was totally spoilt. I can still see Daddy coming into the ward and giving me Mummy's jewel case for my birthday. Inside it was her beautiful diamond solitaire. I think at that time he couldn't give me enough. I have treasured the ring and worn it constantly ever since. It is my most precious possession.

The operation to remove the lower lobe of my left lung took many hours. My bed was taken to the operating theatre to avoid too much moving. I had to be very lightly anaesthetised, and I recall coming round while still on the table. I could hear Mr D'Abreu's urgent voice saying 'Hurry! Hurry!' before I went out like a light again.

In the hospital chit-chat it was always said that doctors and nurses made bad patients; that if things were to go wrong it always seemed to be with them. Whatever is said, things certainly went wrong with me after the operation.

To begin with, all went well. I had a room to myself and before long I was cheerful, laughing and teasing the nurses. In fact I was a model patient. Then after about ten days I lost my sparkle. I became lethargic, with a poor appetite, and just lay in my bed doing absolutely nothing. So much for my reading plans. Mr D'Abreu was off to Europe for a surgical conference and before he left he said to me, 'You mind that you behave yourself while I am away.' I think he was unhappy that I didn't seem too well, and suspected things were going wrong.

I didn't behave myself. In the middle of his second night away I had a rigor so severe that the bed itself was all a-shake. My temperature soared and I was cooking up an empyema, that is, I had pus in the plural cavity. The nurses and doctors didn't know what to do, so they decided to leave me until Mr D'Abreu's return in thirty-six hours.

I could not understand why my parents spent the next night with me, and I kept whispering, 'Go home.' I could only whisper as I was so short of breath. I remember working myself down to the bottom of the bed, thinking I would find more air there. You would think I would have been given oxygen, but this was 1938.

As soon as my surgeon arrived back I was taken up to the theatre for a second operation. I came back to the ward with a second tube in my side, and this and the one already there were to be my constant companions for another nine months.

It was a painful and unhappy time for me, as my right lung refused to expand and fill the cavity created by the removal of the lower lobe of the left lung. I had to have the tubes changed frequently, and each time there would be more pain. My surgeon would say, 'Good! This means your lung is expanding.' But still it did not.

During the time I was in hospital Mr D'Abreu came to see me, but only to note my physical condition. There was no occupational therapy in those days. Then one of the junior doctors said to me one morning, 'What do you do with yourself all day?'

'Nothing,' said I.

'Don't you read?' he said.

'No.'

'Do anything with your hands – knitting or embroidery?'

'No.'

'Right,' he said, 'this has got to stop. Next time I come to the ward I shall expect to see something in your hands.' So, like a good girl I obeyed, and I can see them now: two trolley cloths which I embroidered with poppies in a foretaste of the development of occupational therapy. Certainly my mental attitude started to improve and I began to live again. Before that, I used to look at the window and think that if I were strong enough I would throw myself out and so dispose of my tiresome body.

By July, eleven months after the operation, my surgeon said that he thought there was no alternative but to operate again. None of us was happy about this. A date about ten days hence was fixed. During the preceding weary months Dad would send me to the seaside every now and then and I would stay in a hotel. This was with the hope that the sea air would do the trick and help my lung to expand. For the last six months I had been mobile, driving the car and generally moving around, looking fairly normal, but still with my clinging 'friends' in my side. When the decision to operate was made I was at a seaside place called Barry Island. I remember Aunty, as we called our stepmother, came and spent the day with me and I was very depressed at the news. I was lying on the bed crying and saying, 'I won't be able to fight my way through another operation. I haven't any fight left in me.' Everyone had said it was my stickability and determination that had brought me this far.

Then one day Jean, my youngest sister, came to spend the day with me. She would have been seventeen as she is ten years my junior. We went to the funfair and took a ride on the dodgems. We were having great fun and laughing a lot when suddenly I had an agonising pain in my side. We went back to the hotel and phoned Dad. He came to fetch us and took me straight to Mr D'Abreu at the hospital. He removed the tubes and said, 'Your lung has expanded.'

I didn't believe him. 'Oh yeah,' I said, 'tell it to the marines. How many times have you said that?' But he insisted, and even left the tubes out. And he was right. My lung had expanded and from then on I began to get well.

To me that was a miracle. I was only about five days short of an operation I didn't expect to live through. Good old dodgems. And what a blessing laughter is.

By this time the war had started. I recall the day it was announced over the radio. I was spending the day with a friend, Rita, in Cardiff and I had taken my gasmask with me, which was mandatory. When we heard the news we rushed for our gasmasks as though we were to be bombed immediately! Rita was most concerned for her two large and beautiful dalmatian dogs. She said she must take them immediately to her family estate in the country, and this we did. The dogs were more important than we humans!

For me, I couldn't get back to work quickly enough, so I started to look for another position as matron in a boys' prep school. I went for an interview at a very prestigious school called Sunningdale, a preparatory school for Eton, where a few years later the Duchess of Kent sent one of her boys. In my interview I put the headmaster, Mr Fox, in the picture about my health. He told me he thought I was too young for the job (at twenty-eight) as he had an assistant matron and laundry maid both of whom were considerably older than I was. So we came to a compromise: I would be employed for a term to see if I was strong enough and also for him to see if I was able to cope with the job. I was delighted, and full of hope and confidence. It was a very responsible job, with sixty boys between eight and twelve, and a large staff.

I settled into the job as if it had been made for me. The boys tested me of course, but once they knew they couldn't get away with any nonsense we became the best of chums. I remember on one occasion a boy came to the medicine room. 'Matron,' he said, 'I don't feel well. My throat is sore. Can I lie down?' I looked at his throat and talked with him. 'What class are you in? Do you like it?' When he shook his head and said he didn't, I grinned at him and suggested he go back to class and apologise for being late. He grinned back and went like a lamb. I never really had any problem with discipline – I think it is a gift you either have or don't have. I remember one master being so hopeless at discipline that when he was on duty at mealtime he would ask me to go in with him. I never felt this gift was anything to brag about – I was only thankful that it had been given to me.

After two weeks the headmaster called me to his study to ask how I was getting on and whether I found the job too much physically. I was able to reply that I was loving the job and my body seemed to be behaving well. He said that he was delighted. He had seen immediately that I had a way with the boys, and would I accept the job? That was very good to hear, and it was soon to help me in a very difficult position.

There was the medicine room, then a huge bathroom with ten baths, then the laundry room. There were no doors in between these rooms. One day I was in the medicine room and I heard Miss Ager, the assistant matron, talking from the bathroom to the laundry maid next door. I could hear quite clearly what she was saying.

Glenys (right) as matron at Sunningdale, with Miss Ager.

'Don't worry! I don't expect any trouble from her. She is too young. I will be the matron in all but name. She can be the figure-head. After all, I have been here for years – and know the place inside and out.'

I went to the doorway and called, 'Miss Ager, I would like to see you in my sitting room.'

I was very angry. I 'wiped the floor' with her and had her in tears. When I had finished, I said to her, 'We will go down to the headmaster straight away together and tell him that one of us has to go, and ask which one he would like to stay.' I knew that Miss Ager did not want that, so I said I would give her another chance, but if ever I heard of her being disloyal to me again, I would go straight to Mr Fox. I am glad to say we became firm friends after that, and worked happily together.

The boys would demand my presence at

their sports matches and I went with them whatever the weather. In winter I would shout from the touchline to keep me warm. Many of these happy relationships lasted long after they had left the school, and several times I went to Eton to take one or the other out to tea and we would have fun together.

I was at Sunningdale at the time of the Blitz on London, when the full weight of the German Luftwaffe would come night after night. We were very close to their route so we had plenty of disturbed nights. There was an Anderson shelter in the grounds but the staff decided not to use it. Instead the cubicles and dormitories were emptied and the boys collected in the drawing room of the headmaster's house, which was connected to the school building. They would lie on the floor and we did our best to keep them amused. I would check every cubicle and dormitory to make sure no boy had slept through the alarm. It was an eerie feeling going through this big empty building with the aid of a torch while the thunder of the passing planes roared overhead. I have no idea why we decided to use the drawing room. Fortunately we escaped a direct hit.

At the height of the Blitz in 1941 I was with Gwenda in London. Both of us had been home on holiday in Wales. I had to return to Sunningdale via London, and Gwenda had to go to London for her practical examination in her finals as a medical student. Because we knew it would be pretty grim spending a night in London, I arranged to spend the night with her instead of going straight through to Sunningdale. Dad gave us the name of a quiet London hotel, and we took a train to Paddington Station. On alighting we were told that an air raid warning had sounded but as everyone around us seemed to be behaving normally so did we and took a taxi to the hotel. As we stood on the pavement and looked at our intended hotel, we saw that there was another one next door. Suddenly I said to Gwenda, 'I don't know why, but I don't fancy this one, let's go to the one next door,' which we did.

At the desk I asked if we could be accommodated for one night and the receptionist said we could, but warned us that there was an unexploded time-bomb in the back of the hotel! She said other guests were staying in the front part, so we booked in.

We had dinner and were sitting in the lounge at 10pm when the warning went. No-one seemed to take much notice, saying that it was too early, and they were right. The All Clear sounded quite soon but in the meantime Gwenda and I had gone up to our room to don our siren suits (as worn by Winston Churchill and very much the 'in thing') and returned to the lounge.

Once again the air raid warning went and we had a choice of going down below to the air raid shelter or going up to bed. I told Gwenda that if she was game to go up to bed to try to get a good night's rest then so was I. So upstairs we went and settled into our beds. I told her if anything happened, to get under the bed. A short time later we heard a single plane flying overhead. Before we knew it a stick of bombs was exploding all around us, including one in the road outside our window, which hit a gas main. The gas ignited and a pillar of flame shot up in front of us. Our main concern was to get out quickly, and I can see myself in my pyjamas with my fur coat and siren suit on my arm and my hat perched on my head running along clutching my suitcase. When we got to the top of the stairs everyone else was milling about below. We stopped on the staircase to put on our siren suits, not caring who saw us.

We were directed to a surface shelter in a road not far from the hotel and there we spent the rest of the night. It was a bad night, too, but nothing else happened to us. At daylight, after the 'All Clear' had sounded, we were taken back to the hotel. Up until then I had been pretty calm about it all, but the sight that was before my eyes made my legs turn to jelly. The hotel we had been meant to stay in had suffered a direct hit and there wasn't much left of it. Apartments on the other side of the road had also been hit and we saw beds dangling in the air, but our hotel was untouched.

When Gwenda went for her practical next morning the examining doctor asked her where she had spent the night, and when she told him he said, 'You poor thing.' However, she passed her examinations and became a fully fledged doctor.

What amazed me was what had made me choose the other hotel? What still small voice was I able to pick up that took us to the hotel that was not bombed?

I know what I believe, but others have said to me, 'Why are you so special

that you should be saved? Are others not just as precious to God as you?'
Yes, I believe they are. But I also believe that if one puts one's life daily into
the keeping of God, one establishes 'wavelengths' that the subconscious can
pick up and respond to. It isn't surprising that those who have not experienced this kind of assurance find it hard to accept. 'Chance' and 'luck' are
not words I use. Too many times my life has shown me how one can be
watched over and guided, and I can't believe anything else.

To me it reveals the enormous caring and power available to all who would
claim it and use it. The tragedy is that we fail to avail ourselves of it. Indeed,
we even fail to believe.

I was so happy at Sunningdale, but to my utter dismay my body let me down
again. I would have bouts of feeling dreadfully ill. It would start with icy cold
at the back of my neck, then during the night I would sweat profusely as if
I had malaria. Miss Ager would come into my sitting room and find me
sitting almost in the fire trying to get my back warm. The school doctor sent
me to a Harley Street specialist and when he next came to see me the school
doctor (inadvertently?) left the specialist's letter on the table in my sitting
room. Needless to say, curiosity made me read it and I got quite a shock.
'There is nothing really that can be done for her. It is a tragic case in one so
young.' I didn't like this at all. I didn't feel at all tragic, only determined to
get on with my life. I never did discover why he said it.

The doctor must have shown the letter to the Foxes because Mrs Fox came
to my room and suggested that I go to see a Christian Science practitioner.
She had a friend who had been greatly helped. I said I would go anywhere
and see anyone if I thought it would help, so Mrs Fox arranged for this
woman to see me. I started to learn something about the Christian Scientists,
but in the end my experience and knowledge got in the way and I couldn't
accept the teaching of the sect.

Meanwhile my body told me I would have to give up my lovely job, and I
reluctantly finished at Sunningdale School at the end of the 1941 school year.

CHAPTER SIX

Convalescence and Conversion

I left London and went to stay with my old nursing friend Enid Williams in the mountains of North Wales.

Enid was by now married to Dr Emyr Wyn-Jones. They had a flat in Liverpool and also a beautiful home high above the village of Llanfairtalhairan in northern Wales. From a knoll in the grounds one could see Mt Snowdon, considered a real mountain in Britain but not very high by New Zealand standards.

During these tedious periods of illness I looked on Llety'r Eos, as the house was called, as my second home. Because it was wartime Enid and the two children, Carys and Gareth, lived there all the time, and Emyr, would visit most weekends from Liverpool. It was good to leave the rarefied atmosphere of London and to live once more among friends with the same medical outlook as mine.

After I had been with my friends for about a month Emyr said to me, 'I think, Glen, that you should have your chest explored again; obviously there is something wrong.'

I cautiously asked, 'What do you suggest?'

Emyr said, 'I am a consulting specialist at Wrexham Hospital, and I could get you in there for another Lipiodol X-ray.'

'Not on your life,' I said. 'I am not having another one of those.' And I meant it. But again, I found how pointless it is to say no to the inevitable. Emyr talked me into it. This time it was even more stressful because I had the local anaesthetic too soon so that during the X-ray I felt far more than I should have. The distress was considerable. However, once I saw the X-ray result, I knew that something would have to be done. The upper lobe of my left lung was like a bunch of grapes: the bronchials were full of pockets.

The next step was that Emyr got in touch with Mr Price Thomas, London chest surgeon. Mr Price Thomas was later to operate on King George VI and be knighted for his efforts. He agreed to see me, so I went down to London again, and for the second time became a patient in the Brompton Chest Hospital. Price Thomas said that he would only operate if he knew that my right lung was all right, which meant yet another Lipiodol X-ray! How my heart sank. But the result showed that my right lung was clear, so Price Thomas said he would operate to remove the upper lobe of my left lung. This meant the total removal of my left lung, as the left lung has only two lobes while the right has three.

I was put into a three-bed ward. This was in 1944, and I have a vivid memory of hearing, night after night, bombers flying overhead. Thankfully, by now they were our planes going over to bomb Germany.

The operation appeared to be a success. It was helped by the use of blood transfusion, which was now normal practice during major surgery. It shows what tremendous progress had been made in surgery as a direct result of the needs of wartime, since I had had my first lobe removed in 1938, only six years earlier.

All went well and I was cheeky and cheerful for about ten days, then, as before, I began to be listless and felt poorly. I told the houseman that when this had happened before it turned out I had been cooking up an empyema (pus in the plural cavity) and I felt the same thing was happening again. But the X-rays did not show any trouble so he was not prepared to listen to me. However, I kept on until one day he gave in and brought a trolley to my bedside and told me he was going to look for the pocket of pus I was so sure was there. He stuck great needles into me all over my chest, and wasn't particularly gentle as he thought I was making a fuss about nothing. It was exceedingly unpleasant but I couldn't say anything as I had more or less asked for it. What was worse, he found nothing.

In the middle of the following night I threw a rigor, and once again the bed shook and my temperature soared. The houseman was called from his bed to see me. His first words to me were 'I am so very sorry, Miss Lewis, you were right all the time and I wouldn't believe you.' The wonderful thing about this second time around was the discovery of penicillin. It was administered to me in tablet form, known as M&B, and saved me from another operation. The infection cleared up and soon I was my cheeky self again. The discovery of penicillin was a direct result of the war. It is nice to think that some good came out of all that horror.

I was very grateful for all that had been done for me, and I anticipated that life would be great now, and that no longer would ill-health stop my enjoyment of it. But life was to show that I had been too optimistic.

Some of my months of convalescence were spent at The Knoll, some in Newport with Morgan and Betty, some with Enid in northern Wales and some in Birmingham with my dear friend Bud from Weston-super-Mare days. During my tedious ill-health I had often spent time with Bud and on Sundays we would go to her church, which was Anglican. The vicar was an archdeacon and we called him 'the Ven', short for Venerable, the title given to an archdeacon. Something very special was to happen during this particular visit.

One Monday morning I was lying in bed and Bud brought me my breakfast before going to work. We had been to church as usual the day before. While I was lying there I was suddenly confronted by what could only be described as a blinding light, and it was as if someone spoke to me and said, 'You must join the Anglican Church.' When Bud came up with my tray I said, 'I'm going to join the Anglican Church.'

She looked aghast. 'You can't do that – whatever would your father think?' Dad was a strong Baptist, and in his view the Church of England was dead. She went off to work quite troubled.

But I was calm and confident. I knew that this was not just me as it had never entered my head before. Later that morning I phoned the Ven and told him I was going to become an Anglican. His comment to me was: 'At last! I have been expecting this for some time.' He somehow knew I was coming to believe in the grace of the Sacrament of Holy Communion. He had allowed me to take Communion for some time, which was quite revolutionary in those days. He went on to say, 'Did you know that the bishop is coming next Sunday? I have a group of boys and girls to be confirmed.'

I had not known.

The Ven went on: 'If you are prepared to come and see me for instruction every evening this week, I will present you to the bishop on Sunday to be confirmed.'

So this is what happened. I have little recollection of my confirmation, except that it was an entirely unemotional event for me. It was just something I had to do. Bud told me afterwards that she had found it far more moving than when she was confirmed.

All this happened within a week, and without my dear Dad knowing anything about it! I knew he would be upset and confused. Although he had been brought up Church of England he had no personal experience of the Living God, and imagined that the church was as dead as his faith.

Soon after my confirmation I left Bud to go to my second home in northern Wales to stay with Enid. But before I left I wrote to Dad and told him what I had done. I thought I must give him time to recover from the shock before I went home. When I wrote that letter, I did not know that I would be presenting him with a second shock when I did go home.

It was lovely to be with Enid again. This was 1942 so we were still at war, but in the hills of northern Wales it seemed another world, except for the coupons for food and clothing. Enid kept a cow, and made her own butter and bread. She was a marvellous cook so we never wanted. Due to a medical condition that wasn't diagnosed until many years later, I had an enormous appetite. I was as slim as a lathe, and yet I had this huge appetite. It was quite embarrassing really, as my body seemed to cry out for food that it did not seem able to assimilate. I know Enid was mystified, as were others because I was so thin. When I returned from New Zealand in 1965, Bud had filled her fridge for my visit and couldn't understand why so much food was left over!

During my convalescence at Llety'r Eos, Enid and I would have long talks. One day I told to her I would so love to serve God in a full-time capacity, but with my health record who would look at me? I could not think who to ask. Did she have any ideas? Enid said she didn't, but she suggested we invite the vicar to come up for a cup of tea, and then I could tell him about myself and see what he could suggest.

The vicar came from the village below Llety and we had a long talk. He asked me if I knew anything of St Christopher's College in Blackheath, London. It was a women's theological college, training women to work full time in the Anglican Church. I said I hadn't heard of it; neither had Enid.

'It has been evacuated from London due to the war,' the vicar continued, 'and is now occupying Retreat House in the Cathedral Close in Chester. Perhaps it would be possible for you to see the principal, Miss Avery, while you are in this part of the world?'

How exciting that sounded. It was quite unbelievable that the college should be in Chester, because that was no distance from Llety, and if Miss Avery agreed to see me I could break my journey there on my way home.

The vicar gave me the address and I wrote immediately. Miss Avery wrote back that she would be pleased to see me and that she would meet the train. By this time the doors were flying open so fast that I was quite breathless and very excited. So was Enid and we laughed and chatted it over.

The day arrived and I got down from the train at Chester, to be met by a diminutive woman, who welcomed me kindly and took me back to the college.

'I think it only fair to tell you about my health before you consider me as a student,' I began. 'I am at about the end of my convalescence from a second operation on my left lung. In fact I have no left lung now, but I do expect to be much better without it.'

She thanked me for being so open with her, and then said that as the third term of the scholastic year was about to begin it would not be wise for me to start until September. Then she thought of an idea. Why not go into residence when term began in May, to see if I would be strong enough to cope with the life. She added that if I would like to do that, she was willing to accept me as a student.

I was overjoyed, and so it was arranged. Miss Avery accepted me without any references, and I said yes without any idea of the cost or where the money would come from! It was as though my life had been taken over. The Lord had just picked me up and plonked me down where He wanted me to be.

It is not possible to recall what my thoughts were as I travelled in the train from Chester home to Cardiff. Since I had last seen Dad my life had been turned upside down, with hugely exciting prospects now after a period of wearisome convalescence. It was all right for me living in this new excitement, but what about Dad? I knew that I must have hurt him with my conversion. How would he react to this further blow?

As I travelled, I recalled that Dad had once told us he would give us each £300 when we married. When I got home I would ask him if I could have that money to train. I was not going to marry, but I was going to serve in the ministry of the church. What a nerve I had! But I was like one taken over and I did not question the rights or wrongs of asking for this money. I just did it. Furthermore, bitterly hurt though he was, and showed me, Dad still let me have the money. This more than anything shows what a wonderful man my father was. It would have been so easy for him to say no. By today's standards it is incredible that that amount of money covered the cost of two and a half years' training in a residential training college.

Dad and I had always had a close relationship, even though it was un-demonstrative I just knew that he loved me. After my entry into the Anglican Church he still loved me, but the closeness was gone and he was never able to express interest in my work.

So began a strange period for me. I had become accustomed to being a person in authority and also to working among young men, yet here I was in a tight-knit community of women, all pretty committed to doing well scholastically, and there was also a touch of competition to be holier than thou! It could have been because I am tall and held myself well, but two of the tutors obviously thought I needed taking down a peg or two and they would needle me quite unkindly. We often felt claustrophobic in the high-pressure atmosphere and when it got on top of us we would dress in our best and take ourselves to the Grand Hotel, where we would sit in the lounge and drink a glass of sherry.

One of the things I loved was that we were only a minute's walk from the beautiful Chester Cathedral. We went there daily for prayer but it was the Sunday Eucharist that taught me the wonder of worship: of being taken out

Student at Theological College.

of one's self and lifted high in joy and love and worship. It was there I learnt the value and importance of the Sacrament of Holy Communion and I was to teach that for many years with great conviction.

My second year at college was to see the end of the war and our return to the college premises in Blackheath, London. During the war it had been used by one of the services, so it was in a tired state when we occupied it again. The chapel windows were without glass and boarded up, and it felt cold and barren. However, it was not long before we had it looking like a chapel again, and the time came when we felt it was again a house of prayer.

My tutor was Deaconess Elizabeth Grinling, who had been a novice mistress at St Andrew's House in London but had had to leave on account of ill-health. We became lasting friends.

At one stage as a senior student I took a long weekend away for my health. When I returned I discovered the college in turmoil. The deputy had fallen out with one of the students and the twenty-five women were clearly divided. I could not believe what had happened but after lengthy discussion we sorted out the differences and things calmed down. I had ended up playing a major role in the peace process.

However, I felt dreadful and I went to my tutor to tell her what had happened. I couldn't understand why, but I felt like hitting out – breaking things and shouting and swearing. She told me, 'This is something you will have to prepare for. When you deal with the turbulence of others and settle it, the turbulence can be transferred to you. You will learn to cope with it. I suggest you take yourself off for a walk and get it out of your system.'

This was good advice, which I have never forgotten. She was a wonderful lady.

We were a mixed bunch. There was one particular student I recall. We would meet in one another's rooms for a cup of tea after dinner and this student would go straight to sit on the bit of floor without carpet. Such 'saintliness' had the opposite effect on me: I would immediately head for the most comfortable chair I could find! We were all so different. All of us had given up some profession or other to do this training. Some were teachers with an academic degree. One student had been a Jew, out of the Women's Royal Army Corps, who had been converted to Christianity by reading the books of C.S. Lewis. We remained friends until she died in 1970.

Before our final examinations we all started to apply for jobs. I thought I would like to go as chaplain into the Women's Royal Army Corps and an interview was fixed for me. But the day before the interview I fell down some very steep stairs, head first, and hurt my back. So the visit had to be cancelled and another date fixed. However, before that day arrived, the principal told me that a vicar was wanting a parish worker and he intended to wait until he found the right one. Would I like to apply? I was intrigued by such fussiness so I said I would go for an interview. The vicar took me to his club for lunch, but because women were not allowed into the club proper I had to be entertained in the restaurant especially designed for members to take their womenfolk!

I liked him, Michael Clarke, and he seemed to like me. He took me back to his home, the Rectory of Holy Trinity, Marylebone, London, and showed me around. Then he asked me if I would come and work with him and I said I would. We arranged that I would start in September. I was to live in the basement bedsitting room of the rectory, which I would need to furnish.

Nothing daunted, I went out one day with a friend on our bicycles to a second-hand furniture shop. There we found a round mahogany table, complete with birdcage so the top could be tipped up. It was black on top and quite ugly. My friend knew about furniture and said she was sure that it was a genuine antique and we could scrub the top and remove the black varnish. I bought it for ten shillings, took it back to college on my bicycle, and Anne and I scrubbed it bare. Sure enough, we found a beautiful bowl of mahogany underneath. I still have that table in 1999, and it is now worth many hundreds of dollars. It was quite a find.

And so it went on: searching out and finding cheap furniture for my room. I had to use an orange box as a bedside table, and I took them all back to college to store until I needed them at the rectory.

It was fascinating the variety of jobs the students were finding. Then the final examinations arrived. Tests on the Old and New Testaments, doctrine, church history, psychology, methodology and practical teaching. I passed all the examinations, and felt real pleasure in gaining a first in teaching.

CHAPTER SEVEN

'Only a Woman'

In September 1946 I moved into the basement of the vicarage, which was to be my home for the next two years. Looking back forty-five years later, as I sit in my cosy and attractive unit in New Zealand, I am staggered by my fortitude in those days.

I would not know what to call my home in the basement. It was certainly not a flat, and bedsitter would be too kind a word for it. There was a large room that must have been the original kitchen, with a flagstone floor. Off the main room was a small room containing a shallow sink with a cold-water tap and an ancient gas stove. On the other side of the staircase leading up to the ground floor was another room, not as large as the main room, with a threadbare carpet and a gas fire. It was in this room that I slept, ate my food, did my work and entertained those who wanted to see me. An unused door opened into the outside area, and two barred windows faced a wall about three feet away. That was my view, along with the shoes and legs of people passing by. There was a gate for entry into the area but this was also never used, except, as I discovered, as a relief area for men as they passed by. One particular hot summer's night I had a window open and a gap in the curtain to let in some air, when I saw a man behind the bars grinning at me as he pressed his face against the bars. It gave me a fright and I was glad of the bars! There was no bathroom or lavatory – I had to go up two flights of stairs to reach those.

Why did I persevere with these conditions for two years? It is a good question. But the thing is, this was just after the war, and Marylebone in the heart of London had been badly knocked about so that accommodation, for what I could pay, was almost impossible to find. During the war we had also become very stoical and expected things to be tough and rough, after what we had gone through in the last four years.

I was left under no illusion as to my place as a woman in the parish. There was a school of thought, which dated from St Aquinas, that women were 'unclean' because of menstruation, therefore they should not go into holy places such as the sanctuary. I was not allowed even to clean the vessels for Holy Communion. This task was done by the verger, who set them out and cleared away after the service. My heart used to ache to be able to clean them to make them sparkle before putting them in a worthy resting place.

The vicar had been the headmaster of Repton, one of the leading boys' public schools in England, and he had come to the position of parish vicar without the theological training I had received, and which was in fact the normal requirement for a man wanting to enter the priesthood. Of course he had university degrees, and the prestige of his previous position, but he lacked the study of the Prayer Book, the doctrine, church history and, above all, the training and discipline of the spiritual life.

An example of this was that although the church was just across the road, we did not go there for any morning prayer or worship during the week. I had been trained in this discipline at college and it meant a great deal to me. After I had been in the parish for a few months I asked the vicar if I could have a key to the church so that I could go there each morning to say my prayers. I had a strong belief that a church needed to be prayed in and not used just on Sundays. As well as this, I thought it would be a good thing for people, as they went to their work, to see the vicar also going to his work each morning. Very reluctantly he gave me the key, but he did not come to the church himself.

So began my lonely vigil. Each morning just before 7.00 I would cross the road, enter the church through the vestry door and make my way to the chapel. There, in winter and summer, I would spend an hour praying Matins and my own prayers. Then finally, after about a year, the vicar said to me one day, rather sheepishly, 'Glenys, would you mind if I joined you in morning worship?' I was overjoyed. I had been hoping and praying that this would happen: it would be wonderful to be not alone. Dear Michael: we became good friends despite his inability to think me capable of doing anything but visit the parishioners.

He had a bad back – we called it lumbago in those days – and one day he was unable to get out of bed. It happened to be a Wednesday and we had a Lenten service scheduled at midday. He called for me and said, 'Glenys, I cannot take the service today. I think the only thing we can do is for you to stand on the steps of the church and tell people as they come that there will be no service.'

With my tongue in my cheek I replied, 'Don't you think it possible that I might be able to take it for you?'

He looked utterly staggered at this suggestion, but said, 'Do you really think you can?' He gave his permission, but it was only the once.

My role in that parish was caring for parishioners. I would sit at the back of the church so that I could note if anyone was a stranger or if there was visible loneliness in those who came. I was not ever given anything official to do in any kind of leadership role, not even where Sunday school was concerned. But I did not mind. Obviously the caring work filled my time and gave me a sense of worth. In retrospect it astonishes me that I was so content. I have no memory of ever being hurt. Yet, I had no social life in that parish: the wealthy side never thought of it, and the poor side couldn't afford it.

The only friend I made in that time has remained a friend to this day. Peggy Old is fifteen to twenty years younger than I, but over the years it doesn't seem to have mattered one bit. This has been the case with many of my friends, and indeed, it still is today. Peggy was doing her nursing training in the University College Hospital in London. Today she lives in Gloucester where she enjoys being a guide in Gloucester Cathedral. We write to each other and once a year, on her birthday, I phone and we chat.

Socially the parish was very mixed. At one end of the scale it included Harley Street, where the top English medical specialists had their rooms. Socially they were well beyond the other end of the scale, who lived in quite appalling conditions.

An example of how poor some of the parishioners were was shown to me once when I came to a door up an alleyway. I knocked and the door was opened, but all I could see was the vague outline of a woman and then total blackness. I told her I was from Holy Trinity Church and a voice said, 'Do come in.' I tried to do so, but as it was so dark I tripped and almost fell into this black hole. The voice in the darkness said, 'I am sorry, of course you cannot see a thing.' The woman turned on the light and then said, 'I don't need the light, you see, I am blind.' She was a lovely little old lady who lived in this tiny place and heated it by leaving her cooking stove on. Often when I visited her I would see her eyebrows singed from lighting the ring on her stove. We became friends and she would offer me a glass of something and of course I had to drink it, although the glass was always filthy. But who could blame her? She couldn't see.

My first Christmas in the parish I asked the rector if he would come with me on Christmas Day to give these friends of mine a can of beer and some goodies. He did and I will never forget how my little blind lady laughed. She thought it wonderful that the rector should bring her a can of beer on Christmas Day. The following Christmas Day I had six of these dear people to my own 'hovel' for the Christmas meal. They stayed to listen to the King giving his message on the radio, and they thought it was marvellous. We laughed a lot, I recall.

I had some strange experiences during my stay at the rectory. My sitting room was the last place in the house for the gas main to reach, so when it was very cold and the gas was being used in the rest of the house, my little fire would go down almost to extinction. When that happened I wore my outdoor coat and gloves, but I was quite unable to write. I did my best to keep warm, and rolled up some newspaper and covered it with a piece of material to pin to the bottom of the draughty door.

In the middle of one night – I could not have been very soundly asleep – I heard the *frow-frow* of the paper roll as my door was carefully opened. 'Who's there?' I called out, at which a torch was beamed onto my face. I switched on my bedside lamp and saw, in the doorway, a burglar complete with white gym shoes!

I had always said that if I was faced with a burglar I would burrow to the bottom of the bed. But not a bit of it. I was out of that bed like a shot and I chased him back up the stairs. He flew out the front door and vanished into thin air, leaving me on the doorstep in my nightwear and bare feet. It was very dark so it would have been quite fruitless to chase him further.

By this time I was shaking all over, so I rushed up to the vicar's bedroom and shouted, not quite truthfully now, 'There's a burglar in the house!'

The sleepy voice of the vicar's wife said, 'Who's there? What's the matter?'

I shouted again, 'There's a burglar in the house!' and with that they were soon out of bed! However, there was little to be done – the burglar was well away by this time. The rectory was one of those tall, thin London houses, five storeys high. Bomb damage repairs were in progress and builders had left a ladder against the house. We realised that he must have entered the house at the top and worked his way down. Poor man, he achieved nothing for his efforts as every room was occupied. Even the drawing room had a bed in it as the vicar's mother-in-law was staying.

Another time I had a visit from a young couple who had a babe-in-arms. Enid, my sister, was staying with me for a couple of days. She was fascinated as she watched the drama they presented. They wanted money to get home to Portsmouth on the south coast of England. I cannot recall the tale they told of why they had no money, but it was pitiful and tearful and of course I believed them. I told them I was not permitted to give them money, even if I had it to give, but then I suddenly had a brainwave. I would phone the police station and ask the police if they could help. The police were most helpful, saying that if I took the couple to the station they would provide them with tickets to Portsmouth.

The young couple thanked me warmly for my help and I directed them to the police station, which was quite close. I saw them to the door and said goodbye but there must have been some suspicion in my mind because I rushed downstairs, put on a hat to hide my face and followed them. Needless to say, they did not go near the police station. When I returned, Enid told me that she had spoken to them while I was on the phone, and had told them she thought it was not good enough that folk like them should come to her sister for money as I hardly earned enough to keep myself alive!

One day I answered the front doorbell of the vicarage and a woman asked if she could speak to me. I took her downstairs to my room, where she poured out some pathetic story. All I remember is that she had no money to buy food. I told her I could not give her money, but could give her something to eat. She accepted my invitation, so I went to my larder to get what I could. It was just after the war so we were still severely rationed, but I gave her all I had and as she ate it I could see that she was really hungry.

After she finished eating I told her if she went home to get her ration book and came back we could go together to the store and I would pay for some more food for her. She thanked me warmly and set off but I never saw her again; I have no idea why. Perhaps she was not accustomed to trusting people so she was afraid that I might have contacted the police in her absence. I do not know. There was one outcome of this story, though. I had not told any-one about what happened, yet after that my larder did not remain empty. People came with gifts and said things like, 'I thought you could do with this,' or 'Here's a little gift in case you are running short.' It was a marvellous feeling of God's caring love coming to me through my friends.

Often when I had some spare time I would visit Central Deaconess House, Hindhead, Surrey, a quite lovely part of the English countryside. These visits introduced me to the Anglican Deaconess Order, which has been restored in the Church of England in the last century from the ancient Order of Deaconesses that flourished in the sixth century under Bishop Chrysostum in Constantinople. Then there was also a permanent Diaconate for men, and the ordination for men and women was identical. The cross worn by deacon-esses in the twentieth century was a copy, in silver, of the cross on the gatepost of the Deaconess House there.

At the time I came to know of the order it was struggling to stay alive as there were few women coming forward. There was nothing much to attract them; and you would have needed a strong sense of vocation and commit-ment even to consider it. The 'uniform' was incredibly out of touch with the present day. It was halfway between a Catholic nun's black habit and normal dress. Most people recognised the habit of a nun, but the long dark blue half-dress half-habit, complete with a dark blue veil left people mystified. Who were these women? Back then the status of ordained women was largely unknown as their position and duties were very curtailed.

During the time I was in the parish in London I began to get the old familiar 'inner pushes' towards a life of service. This time I fought them quite strongly – I had no wish to go about looking like a fuddy-duddy. But the push became so strong that finally I gave in and offered myself for training as a deaconess in the Church of England. I was accepted and left the parish at the end of 1948. I was not really sorry to go. The vicar's parting shot was: 'If you are ordained a deaconess, you cannot expect to return here. I would not have a deaconess on my staff.' This did not surprise me as his male chauvinistic attitude to my work in the parish had already been revealed to me.

CHAPTER EIGHT

Serving God 'Out There'

And so I was off to Gilmore House, Clapham Common, London, for six months. There were about twenty women students at the Deaconess Training House studying for the qualification I had already gained at St Christopher's College, preparing to work for the church in a lay capacity. Therefore I did not have to study for examinations, but I was to imbibe the 'ethos' of the order. Perhaps I appeared too worldly? Certainly, I used cosmetics and had the occasional cigarette!

While I was at Gilmore House I made some good friends. Pam Rhodes was one, and to relate this amusing incident (not amusing at the time), I will have to tell you a bit of her background. When Lord and Lady Plunket were killed in an air disaster in the 1920s their two young sons came to live in Pam's home as her mother was Lady Plunket's sister. The elder of the two sons became Lord Plunket after his father's death and at the time of my visit to Pam's home he was an equerry to the Queen. When Pam invited me to her home for the weekend she probably didn't know – or if she did she wouldn't have thought anything of it – that Lord Plunket was having a house party.

At drinks before dinner I was introduced to about twelve young people, only to find that each and every one of them was a lord/lady in his/her own right. I was hopelessly out of my depth already but worse was to follow. When we went to dine, I was faced with a dining table large enough to seat us all, beautifully equipped with shining crystal and sparkling silver.

I could possibly have coped, had I not been given the seat of honour at the right hand of Lord Plunket! This meant that I was the first to be served at each course and expected to know what to do – but I didn't! It was a nightmare. Thankfully, on my right was Pam's very kind uncle, who surreptitiously showed me the way.

By the time we went back into the drawing room I was very quiet and pretty miserable, but dear Pam came to my rescue without saying a word. She went up to the huge fireplace, where logs were burning brightly, turned her back to it, lifted up her long dress at the back and, with legs astride, proceeded to warm her posterior! We both roared with laughter and I relaxed and enjoyed the rest of the evening.

When Pam finished her training at Gilmore House she visited New Zealand to see her brother. Shortly after that she became a parish worker with Archdeacon Woods in Christchurch. She was much loved as she went around the parish in an open two-seater car with her large dog beside her. Eventually the Mothers' Union in South Africa invited her to join them, which she did. I will be referring to Pam later in these memoirs, as it was she who began the action that brought me to New Zealand in January 1960.

While I was at Gilmore House the depth of my commitment became obvious. One example of this has a funny side. I was a regular visitor to St Andrew's House in London, a convent of nuns who were also ordained deaconesses. (Their story is to be found in *The Deaconess* by Janet Grierson.) The Mother Superior, Mother Clare, and I became friends. I found myself getting what I thought was another 'inner push' from God to offer myself as a nun. I was actually staying at the Convent when it came to a head, and I thought I must see Mother Clare and tell her. Before the time came for me to see her, I shed a few tears as I took off my mother's ring, which I had worn for many years, and said goodbye to other such 'worldly goods' which I cherished. The time came for me to go and see Mother Clare and tell her what was happening inside me. When I finished, her face lit up with a lovely smile and with half a chuckle she said to me, 'My darling Glenys, your vocation is not in a convent, your vocation is "out there" in the world. You have a real gift for getting alongside people, and it is there that you will fulfil your ministry.'

She was right and I came to accept her wisdom, but it was quite difficult to begin with. In a strange way I had felt 'free' after I had given away my possessions and I did not find it easy at first to take them on board again. But in my heart I knew she was right and many times afterwards we would have a chuckle together at the thought of Glenys the nun.

Central Deaconess House at Hindhead in Surrey was a house for deaconesses to go and stay in for holidays or retreat before ordination. I had a three-week retreat there before my ordination. It was lovely – a lovely chapel and beautiful surroundings.

Almost next door to this house lived the head deaconess of the Guildford Diocese. Edith Banks was an elderly woman, badly crippled with arthritis and very wealthy. She had been doing the work without a stipend, and only part time, but she felt that the time had come for the diocese to have a full-time head deaconess, who would also be the secretary of the Diocesan Council for Women's Ministry in the Church. This would mean the overall care of all the women who worked for the church full time in the diocese. There were about thirty women involved, including Church Army Sisters, a diocesan organiser of Sunday school work, moral welfare workers, a diocesan organiser of the same, and so on. The position would also entail a lot of public speaking and preaching. She asked me to apply.

I was overwhelmed and doubted whether I could take on such a job. I wasn't even ordained as a deaconess, and yet here they were, asking me to take on the job of licensed head deaconess and secretary of the Guildford Diocesan Council for Women's Ministry in the Church on the very day I was to be ordained. Incredible!

While all this was going on the bishop and Edith Banks approached the standing committee of the diocese for funding for the position but their request was turned down. There was no way they could consider such an appeal. However, the bishop and Edith did not give up easily and between them they approached enough individuals to provide sufficient money to enable them to make the appointment. Eventually, of course, the diocese was forced to take on the payment of my stipend. This was the first of three times in my life when standing committees – one in England and two in New Zealand – refused to give money for the appointment of a woman as an official of the diocese. Yet the money was found privately and the appointments were made. In those days it was not easy for women to find work at a parish level, but to be a diocesan official was quite beyond the pale.

The day arrived for me to be ordained a deaconess and licensed as head deaconess of the Guildford Diocese. It was to be held in Holy Trinity, the pro-cathedral while the new cathedral was being built. It was a moving and intimidating experience for me as really I knew nothing of the position or the work to which I was being licensed. It was especially moving as it was the last official act that John, the Bishop, was to take before his retirement. All too soon he was gone and I was so sorry as he had been very caring over the whole business of my appointment. Soon after, Bishop Henry Montgomery-Campbell arrived. As he was already a bishop he did not have to be consecrated but he had to be enthroned and he preached at the service in the cathedral.

The time came for the head deaconess to meet the new bishop and a time was made for me to go to Farnham Castle, where he lived, for my appointment. I was shown into a large room and announced. The bishop was sitting at his desk, with his back to me, facing the window which had a fantastic view. He uttered not a word and remained sitting, leaving me high and dry. Without turning around he called out, 'Sit down.' No way was I going to sit down! How rude of him! So I remained standing. Eventually he came toward me and we both sat down. Neither of us knew what to say to the other. In my nervousness I blurted out, 'I was at your enthronement last Sunday and I thought you preached a very good sermon'.

'Oh! Did I?' he said with arched eyebrows, looking distinctly cynical. I blundered on, 'Yes, you told us you began your ministry in August 1911. But, you left out the most important event in August 1911 – I was born in August 1911!'

What a nerve, but he loved it and roared with laughter. The ice was broken and we became genuine friends. I have found over and over again that laughter does this, and I have used it many times in sermons, public speaking to break the ice when facing antagonism. It always works.

How do I recall and write of those ten years? I can but 'moither' over the time. You may recall that when I worked in the parish in London the vicar would not permit me into the sanctuary or to care for the communion vessels. This will give you some idea of the position women had in the church forty years ago. But I had about thirty full-time women working in the diocese under my care, performing all sorts of functions. I would keep in close touch with them, arrange meetings with them, be the go-between if the bishop or a vicar wanted a worker. Sometimes a vicar for whom I had arranged a deaconess would come to see me and say, 'This woman is no good at all. Get rid of her, and I don't want another one. I would come back at him and say, 'But if you had a deacon, and he was no good, you wouldn't go to the bishop and say "This deacon is no good, I don't want another one."' This shows the great obstacles we faced in gaining acceptance of women into the ministry. And then of course their ministry within a parish was very nebulous. They were really only allowed to do lay work – running the Sunday school, organising meetings – things anybody could have done.

None of them was allowed to occupy the pulpit – that high honour was reserved to me as head deaconess. I made full use of it and I was frequently asked to preach in one church or another throughout the diocese. It was very rewarding work. One Sunday I was preaching in Bramley, where there was a lovely old church, and after the service the verger came up to me and said, 'I must tell you how much I enjoyed your sermon. It is the first I have been able to hear for a long time.' I came to realise that I had this gift: I enunciate clearly and my voice carries well. It has stood me in good stead.

But every other woman had to stand on the chancel steps if she was going to speak in the church. It was absolutely monstrous. It was obviously going to be a step-by-step process.

With the title I carried you would have thought I was a very important person in the diocese, but alas, not much thought was given to how I lived. I was provided with a car to get me around the diocese, and it was nicknamed the Red Devil because it was black with a red interior. But my stipend was pretty poor and I could not afford to rent a flat, and so I lived in a sequence of bed-sitters, which did not give one much privacy or space. Looking back, I am amazed that I did not grumble or complain at the paucity of my living quarters, both in London and in Guildford, and also that no-one in authority showed any concern or interest.

I was very involved with the dean of the cathedral for a couple of years in a 'Wake Up Churchgoers' campaign. It was based on a study of communism and the devotion and commitment of communists. The dean wrote several booklets on this topic, which were the subject of weekly study by groups of men and women. This exercise was highly successful in increasing people's devotion and commitment.

Weekend conferences on the same subject also created a real fellowship among us. We would have really tip-top men coming to them. I remember two men I wanted to invite because they were super chaps. Their wives agreed to come but there was no way they were going to. They said, 'What are we going to do if we can't have our glass of sherry before dinner?' I said, 'That's no problem – bring your sherry and I will join you!' In the end they came and we had such fun, because all five of us would get out our tooth mugs and drink our sherry. We were always late going in to dinner and nobody knew why!

In 1949 there were still areas of suffering after the war. One of these was a home in Guildford for displaced children. Early in the war when London was getting a dreadful battering from air raids, it was decided that children should be evacuated to the countryside. It must have been thought a good thing to do, although in hindsight one is able to see how cruel it was, as many never saw their families again.

Anyway, the matron of the home sent out a request for men and women in Guildford to offer to be an uncle or aunt to one of the children, as they had no family. When I heard of this I was appalled and phoned the matron to offer. I was rash enough to say, 'If you have a difficult girl, I will become her aunt, because she probably has character and great need.' The matron replied, 'I've got just the one for you,' and laughed.

With trepidation I went to collect Barbara to take her out for the afternoon. I do not recall what we did but we ended up in a café having tea with a plateful of rich cream cakes before us. She had a good tuck in, but conversation was difficult. I ended by saying, 'Barbara, if you would like, I will be your aunt, and your friend. I will take you out and we will do things together. Would you like that?'

She shrugged her shoulders and said nothing. So I asked her again, and she replied, 'You can if you want to, but you won't last.'

That was a fatal thing to say to me, because I like a challenge. It was hard work and I did not enjoy it one bit. One day after taking her out I was driving her home when we saw two other girls from the home climbing the hill. I stopped and gave them a lift. When we arrived, the two got out of the back, both thanking me profusely for the lift, while my Barbara just picked up the parcels lying on her lap, said 'Bye' and walked away without a smile.

No doubt about it, she had character and was bright with it. I held on like a limpet. In the years ahead she had some difficult times but I was there for her and we eventually came to love each other. We are still in close contact. Barbara has been to New Zealand twice since I retired. When I came to New Zealand she started calling me Mum or Mother in her letters, and signing herself 'Your loving daughter'. Of all I did in my ten years in Guildford, I think the best and most rewarding was when I accepted the matron's challenge to become an aunt to Barbara.

One day in 1958 I was called home as my father was dying. When I went into his bedroom I was greeted with a wonderful smile. He was delighted that I was there. He died the next day but I have a lovely warm recollection of the evening before. My stepmother and I were playing cards in his room, as he had no desire to talk, and we both looked over to him at the same time. He blew a kiss to both of us and looked so peaceful and happy to have us there.

After his death he was placed in his coffin in the dining room for the days before his funeral. I remember he was dressed in pyjamas and a silk dressing-gown, and he looked so young and peaceful, although he was eighty-five when he died. We found ourselves going into him and saying, 'Hello, Dad!', almost expecting him to get up and join us. I found I couldn't grieve for him, although he had been a wonderful father, like a rock, always there for us.

Back in Guildford one day I was walking up the hilly High Street when a clergyman overtook me and said, 'Goodness, what is the matter with you? I couldn't believe it was you I saw, I thought it was an old woman!' I did feel quite dreadful, so I took myself to the doctor and twenty-four hours later I was admitted to hospital, with a sub-cutaneous glucose drip in my arm.

CHAPTER NINE

Detour to India

After two or three days in hospital my doctor said, 'I am afraid this has to be faced. I am going to have to put you off work for three months.' This was in the winter of 1954. Apparently they had discovered that my body does not absorb sugar. This led to a deficiency of glucose in the bloodstream, known as hypoglycemia.

'Have a heart,' I said, 'Whatever will I do with myself for all that time in this dreadful weather?' To which he replied that he knew it would be tough but I would cope!

One of the first people I told was Helen Douglas. She was a widow, living in a lovely home in Wonersh, a beautiful village close to Guildford. She was involved with our activities at the cathedral and we had become very close friends. Helen was horrified. 'There is only one thing for it,' she said. 'You will have to get away from here and find the sun!' I burst out laughing. How was I going to go gallivanting overseas when I had only about sixpence in the bank? It was a good joke. I was earning very little in those days and so I could see myself confined to visiting friends' homes, hugging their fires and doing my best to be cheerful for three months.

Not long after this Helen came to see me and told me the most fantastic news. Since she had last seen me, she had told all my friends of my situation and her conviction that I should go and find the sun. My friends had all agreed and donated enough money to send me on a cruise! Aboard the Union Steamship Company ship *Warwick Castle*, first class, I was to sail through the Mediterranean, down the east coast of Africa to Cape Town, then back up the west coast of Africa and back to England. The cruise would last two months. I was speechless. What could I say to such generosity, such caring? It made me want to dance and sing with gratitude. I hugged Helen, scarcely able to contain my excitement.

When you work and earn very little you get used to accepting gifts – big gifts – because people are very kind. But suddenly I came back to reality. 'Helen,' I said, 'That is wonderfully generous of you all, but I am afraid I cannot accept. To travel first class I would need a new wardrobe, and that I cannot produce.'

A broad smile lit up Helen's face. 'I know,' she said, 'and I have the answer to that as well. A friend of mine has just returned from Rhodesia where she has been visiting her daughter. She travelled first class and has a wardrobe of sundresses, evening dresses, cocktail dresses – in fact all that you will need for first-class travel on a liner. She is about the same build as you and she is happy to lend them to you if they fit.'

I was overwhelmed. Who could hope for such a friend? Immediately I was anxious to try on the clothes. That was soon arranged, and every garment fitted as if it was made for me.

Next was all the excitement of getting my passport up to date and the necessary injections for overseas. As I was not too well, and as it would have been necessary for me to go to London for one of these injections, the doctor suggested that I wait and have them all at Mombasa en route. If only we had foreseen the outcome of that decision.

I was staying with Helen, and the day before I was to embark a cable came from India to say that my sister Gwenda, who was an anaesthetist in Vellore Hospital in south India, was very ill with poliomyelitis. I couldn't believe it. 'That settles it,' I said, 'I cannot possibly go on a cruise with Gwenda so ill in India.'

But Helen was rational and sensible, and answered, 'What can you do for Gwenda sitting here in England? That will be no good at all, so you must continue your plans and get yourself well again.' So the next day I left Guildford for Southampton where we were to embark. Helen had warned me that when I first lined up to go on board I would look at my fellow passengers and think, 'Heavens, am I going to be stuck with this lot for two months?'

But she had reassured me that I would soon find friends among them and thoroughly enjoy myself. I was thankful for that warning, as she was right on both counts! I did meet people whom I liked and to whom I responded well. I was very thankful to them as it was daunting going on a cruise all alone.

It was a lovely liner – not too big, so it was easy to get to places without having to walk miles. I had a port-side cabin to myself, and I was fortunate to find a friend in a doctor's wife who was visiting her daughter in Kenya. We made friends with the captain and the purser, and went to cocktail parties in the captain's quarters. It was all quite wonderful. I had always dreamed of going on a cruise as I love the sea, but had never thought it would actually happen. Yet, here I was, swimming in the pool, watching the moonlight on the water, playing deck games, lazing in the sun, dancing at night and eating fabulous food. All this with fun people. It was great to have a ship's pal. We could do all sorts of things together that are not so easy to do alone.

When we stopped at Genoa a friend and I went to a place called San Rafael where we had lunch al fresco, in the sunshine. Neither of us knew anything about ordering wine, but we looked at the wine list and I said, 'Ooh, I like the sound of Santa Marguerita.' So we ordered a bottle of Santa Marguerita. We didn't order a small bottle – oh no, we had the full-sized bottle! We were drinking it away there, and we weren't really getting tipsy – it was absolutely lovely but we thought we had better come to a stop. Sitting at the table next to us were a husband and wife and daughter from the ship. He was what you would call a 'Bla-Bla Britisher' and he had been throwing his weight around a bit on the ship. I turned to him and asked him if he would like to finish our wine for us. He said he would be delighted. So he poured it into his glass, lifted it to his lips and said, 'By Jove, you really have had the pick of the wine list!' You can imagine how tickled we were. We went out to the jetty and had a good laugh.

Although they were happy times, in a very real sense I was being torn apart. One side of me was revelling in this wonderful trip, which was all I had hoped it would be – full of sun and sea, fun and fellowship and lots of laughter – while the other side of me couldn't forget Gwenda so very ill in India. Feeling troubled one particular day, I went to my cabin to turn it over to the Power.

I shed tears as I toyed with the idea of asking the captain for a refund of the cost of the remainder of the cruise so that I could leave the ship at Aden and fly to India. I decided that if the money could be refunded I would accept that it was right for me to leave the ship and go to India, but if the money could not be refunded I would also know it was right for me to stay on board and enjoy myself.

Having made that decision I went to see the captain. I told him the whole saga and when I had finished he looked at me sadly and said, 'I am very sorry but the firm policy of the company is that at no time can money be refunded en route.' I accepted that and turned to go but he stopped me, saying, 'But there is no harm in trying. We will send a cable to England. I suggest you go to the purser. Tell him that I have said to send a cable to the office in London and that both of you are to make it as heart-rending as you can!' So the purser and I compiled the cable with much fun and enjoyment and sent it off. The reply came back: 'Refund the money.' So there I was. I had asked for a decision, and the decision was made. I was to leave the ship at Aden and go on to Gwenda in India. I had very mixed feelings about this. The thought of leaving the ship and travelling on my own to India was quite terrifying. I was also having the most wonderful time on board the ship, but I felt that I needed and wanted to go to Gwenda. My course was set and preparations had to begin for me to leave.

From then on I was in a bit of a whirl and left all the organisation to the captain. All I had to do was pack and be ready to leave the ship at Aden on the Sunday morning. There was much regret shown by my new friends and the leave-taking was quite painful for me. We dropped anchor well out and a tugboat brought out the agent who would be looking after me. When the captain said goodbye to me he handed me a large bundle of English sterling, more money than I had ever held before. Clutching it tightly in my hot little hand I left the ship with the agent and my luggage. He took me to a hotel that overlooked the harbour and I could see my *Warwick Castle* standing there.

Before the agent left he said, 'You realise it is Sunday. There will be no banks open, nowhere to deposit this large sum of money you have. I have been making enquiries as I understand that you want to fly to India. There are two options open to you. There is a plane going out to India tonight, a specially chartered flight for Indian workmen who are returning to India, and there is one cancelled seat on the plane. It goes out at midnight. Or you can wait here in Aden until I can get you a booking on a normal flight.'

I thanked him and said that I would take the flight that night, as I did not want to hang about in Aden.

'Right,' he said, 'then I will confirm the booking I made. There is one problem though: the money. I think it would be inadvisable for you to take so much cash into India. I suggest you hand it over to me and I will give you my card with the amount written on it. Of course you must keep enough for your own personal use.'

Somewhat dubious but with few options, I said, 'Well, I guess you know best,' and handed over the money. In exchange he gave me his card with the sum written on the back and the words 'Received from Glenys Lewis'. To this day I have no idea how much he paid for the hotel or for my ticket to India. All I know is that when I was arranging my return trip to England, by plane to Ceylon then by ship to England, the money that was forwarded from Aden, was just enough.

In retrospect it is all so astounding. Here was I taking a cancelled seat on a specially chartered plane leaving in the middle of the night for Bombay, about 800 miles north of Madras, the nearest city to where I wanted to go. I had no idea how I was going to get from Bombay to Madras. How did I think I was going to cope on a small plane filled with Indian workmen for eighteen hours? And how I could have given all that money to a complete stranger? I must have been in a mental limbo. As I stood in the hotel grounds and waved to my ship as she sailed away, I felt desperately lonely and very scared.

After a rest in my hotel room and dinner, the agent called for me at about 11.30pm and took me to the airfield where I boarded the plane. I discovered I was the only woman, and the only white person apart from the pilot. The steward was a large African whose chief duty seemed to be to dispense large mugs of very hot, very strong, *very* sweet tea.

We travelled through the night and at dawn we landed on a small island off the coast of Arabia. The pilot whisked me off to have breakfast in the Officers' Mess of the Royal Air Force, where I was right royally treated! But what nearly finished me was finally getting a look at the plane I had flown in all through the night. The pilot, who was ex-RAF had bought it from the RAF and was running charter flights to make a living. It looked ready for the rubbish-tip.

It took us a whole day to fly across the Arabian Sea. To begin with we went over the Arabian Desert and I have never seen anything so stark and terrifying. I was very thankful when, early in the evening, we landed in Bombay.

I had sent a cable to Gwenda from Aden, saying, 'Left ship, flying to India, see you soon. Glen.' That was all. I had not said what plane I was travelling on, or where I was arriving in this vast continent of India. I didn't know myself! Before we landed in Bombay one of the workmen came up and asked if I was travelling with a camera. I asked him why and he said that he had two cameras with him and that customs allowed only one per person. I said that I was sorry but I did have a camera with me, so we smiled at each other and he returned to his seat. A few moments later another approached me and asked if I was carrying any gramophone records. It seemed he had two boxes of ten and customs allowed only one box. I had to admit that I was not carrying any records, so he asked if I would mind taking one box through customs. I agreed, and suggested he write my name on the box, which he did. I never saw his box of records again, so somehow he must have retrieved it from my baggage.

Of course I had not yet had my inoculations, as I'd never got as far as Mombasa. When my passport was examined in Bombay and it showed this up, all hell broke loose. I was ushered into a wire cage in the centre of the airport where I had to stay. Folk passing by must have wondered what rare type of wild beast was on display! Remembering my horror of travelling alone, you may be able to enter into my feelings at this time. I was terrified. Whenever anyone came near I asked to see the British consul, but to no avail.

Eventually they took me out of the cage and escorted me through the airport, thoroughly spraying me as we went. They took me to a van that was heavily draped with mosquito nets. By this time it was dark and I was taken through the night without any idea of where I was going. By this time I was a nervous wreck and kept muttering, 'Where are you taking me?,' but I have no recollection of a definite answer.

To me it seemed a long way before we got to our destination, which was an isolation hospital. I was taken along a corridor where the window space was heavily draped with mosquito nets to a room that I was to occupy for ten – or was it fourteen? – days. I had no glass to the window and no door in the doorway, so I felt very exposed and very frightened.

Come daytime, I found I was the only patient. I had a nursing sister to look after me, a 'boy' who looked about forty years old, and a doctor who came to see me every day. It eventually became clear that he did not come to see after my health so much as to have a game of billiards with me! Here was I, forty years after my father had taught Enid and me to play billiards as children, able to give the doctor a good enough game for him to travel out to the hospital from Madras each day for a game! Even the morning I was leaving he came to play a game of billiards, and I nearly missed my train because he was so reluctant to finish.

As far as possible I was given 'English' food, and I remember the chicken was very tough and unappetising. The sister was horrified one day when she saw me lift a deckchair and take it from my room into the corridor, and she told me I should have asked the 'boy' to move it for me. Later we were chatting and she was telling me how much she wanted to go to London. I said to her, 'Do you ever make your own bed? Do you do your own washing or cooking or cleaning?'

She was appalled. 'Certainly not!' she said. 'I have plenty of people to do that for me.' So I told her that if she wanted to go to England she would have to learn to do all of those things for herself. I tried to explain what the situation was like in Europe for everyone after the war. I have no idea if she ever got there.

Although at the time my incarceration seemed ghastly and an awful waste of time, it was in fact a real blessing. I had not told the authorities in Vellore that I was coming. and if anyone knows the vast continent of India, they will know that it is a vast distance between Madras and Vellore, and I was not even in Madras! Looking back, I wonder what would have happened to me had I gone through customs in the normal way. I would have had to deal with the currency, the hotels, the airport, the railways, and all alone. I did not know anyone to whom I could have turned. I would have been utterly and completely lost. Instead, and that is what is so wonderful about being 'kept by the Power', I was put into this isolation hospital. I was looked after, and I was able to phone the hospital in Vellore and tell them what had happened. That enabled them to organise my travel arrangements from that end.

When eventually I left the hospital I took a train to Bombay. I will never forget that train because I had never before seen so many people. The train was packed – they were literally sitting on the roof, hanging off the side. In Bombay I was met by a man and woman who were missionaries. They took me to their home and introduced me to some of the beauty spots of Bombay. I spent the night with them and next day they took me to the airport and saw me onto the plane to Madras.

I had no concept of the vastness of the Indian continent until I took that flight, and no idea of the distance between Bombay and Madras. Again the folk at Vellore had arranged for me to be looked after, and in Madras I was met by another missionary and given hospitality for the night. On my own I would have been completely lost amid the literally thousands of people all milling around. I wouldn't have known what to do. Instead I was met at the airport, spent the night with them, and then taken to the station.

The train journey to Vellore the next day was quite an experience. I was put into a carriage that was like a very small room. On one side were two bunks, and on the other side there was one. Two men occupied the two bunks while I had the single one. We were friendly in a smiling kind of way, but I do not recall being able to speak with them. One was more smartly dressed in a suit than the other. He took his shoes off and left them neatly on the floor. During the journey we saw a stream of water appearing under the door from the toilet, and the man seemed mesmerised by this as the water came nearer and nearer to his shoes. In the end he rescued them and took them up beside him!

After about four hours the train arrived at the station where I had to disembark for Vellore, and I was met by a group of people from the hospital. There was much excitement as they gave me news of Gwenda. She was still very ill, but they were thankful to be able to say that she wasn't in an iron lung. It had been thought it would be necessary and an iron lung had been brought from Madras in readiness. Although she was paralysed from her neck down, the wonderful thing was that her diaphragm continued to work, so she could still breathe.

There was much whispering of 'Here she comes!' as I was taken down the corridor to see my darling sister. And there she was. Sitting up in bed, supported by pillows, very white in the face but with a light in her eyes and a smile on her lips. That was reward enough for me. Who would have believed that such a miracle could be possible? I could only feel so strongly that I was being 'kept by the Power'.

After spending a little time with her I was taken to Gwenda's quarters in the big bungalow on the campus. As in the isolation hospital in Bombay, I found it all very strange. All my life I had been accustomed to glass in the windows

Glenys, visiting Gwenda in hospital, chats with Dr Jacob Chandy and Rev Ganjeye Sanyuaryar.

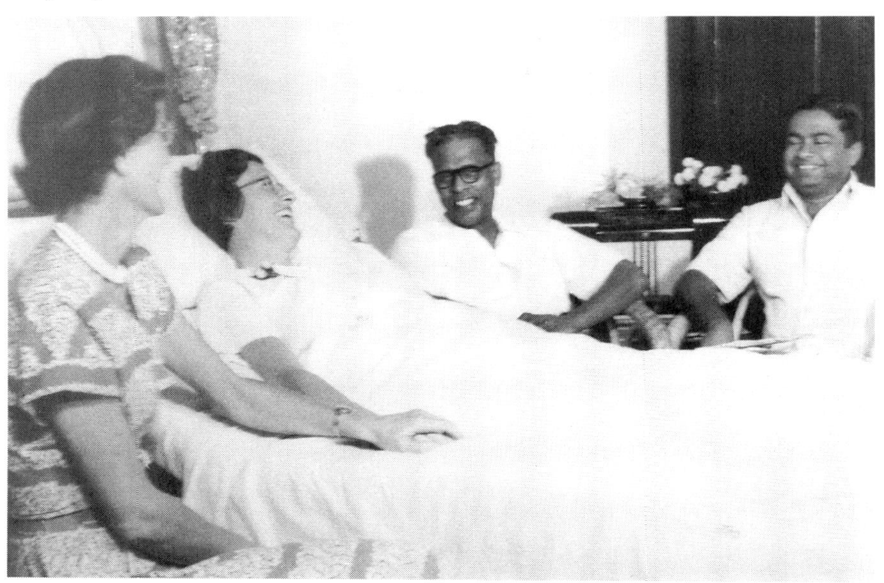

and a door in the doorway. Yet, here I was with open spaces for windows and a curtain for a door. Gwenda had an en suite to her bedroom, if you could call it by so grand a name. There was a shower, a basin and a type of loo I had never met before. There was nothing to sit on; one had to 'tubby' down over an area with a plug in the floor. I am glad all this happened when I was young as I could not do that today – I would never be able to get up again!

I had my meals with the medical staff in the big bungalow. Most of the staff were missionaries from America, Britain and Canada and I was soon made to feel at home. In fact I was thoroughly spoilt, not only by these kind people but also by all the staff of the hospital, whatever department they were in. It was obvious how affected they were by Gwenda's illness, and it also became apparent to me how much they liked and admired her.

I recall vividly that as soon as Gwenda was well enough she was taken to the hospital therapy pool. She had to be taken on a stretcher as at that time she was unable to move her limbs. The porters who put her on the trolley treated her like Dresden china and, as they wheeled her to the pool, they did it very slowly so as not to bump her in any way. It was very touching to witness their loving care of her. I went with her, put on my bathing dress and joined her in the water. To keep her afloat she had a rubber ring under her head, and another under each foot. We made a fun exercise of this and laughed a lot.

When I was not with Gwenda, people were very kind and took me around. One day I was taken to the Leprosy Centre, some miles away from the hospital. Here I think I should say something about Dr Paul Brand. One of the tragedies of leprosy patients was the deterioration of the tendons in the palm of the hand. The result was that the hands become claws and therefore quite useless. Paul Brand had devised the operation whereby the tendons from the back of the hand were transferred to the palms. The results were quite dramatic: the hands became usable again and the patients were taught skills in the occupational therapy department.

By the time I visited the unit all this was well developed and I was able to watch both men and women learning to use their hands again: carving, pottery, weaving, anything to make things that could later be sold. The effect on the patients can be imagined. From being men and women – and, yes, children – of despair and hopelessness, they became eager, full of renewed hope and happiness.

Another time I was taken out with the travelling eye hospital. This was a bus converted into a day hospital. We travelled many miles into the depths of the country, to a spot well known by the locals, who would walk fifty miles or more to be seen by the doctors. The doctors and nurses would set up an outpatients' clinic there on the roadside, in the open. People would already be there waiting with oriental patience, while others would continue to arrive through the day. In the 1950s when I was there, eye disease was a scourge attacking men, women and children. It was obvious how much this care and treatment was valued: one had only to look at their faces to see the expectation and relief that something was being done.

I was filled with admiration at the resourcefulness of the hospital authorities. As a hospital-trained nurse from the West, I had thought of hospitals always as buildings. Yet, here in India the hospital also went to the people in their need. I could not help wishing, and I still do, that this caring outlook could be found in the hospitals of the Western world.

One day a woman I came to know as 'Aunt Ida' told me she was going to take me to visit a family much honoured in Vellore. She told me to behave myself in that whatever was offered to me in the way of food or drink I was to accept with grace and thanks. She warned me that what might be offered could seem strange and unappetising. I told her not to worry, that when I was a parish worker in London I used to visit a blind woman who was a darling but could not see to know whether her glasses or cups were clean when she offered me a drink, but that I never refused. I went with her to this home and although I did find everything strange, I did not disgrace myself, according to Aunt Ida.

I cannot mention 'Aunt Ida' without writing something about this marvellous woman. Dr Ida Scudder was in her eighties when I had the joy of meeting her. She was the daughter of missionaries from America who had worked in Vellore. Ida was sent back to America to be educated and was quite adamant she would never be a missionary. She, like many of us, was to learn that it is not wise to say 'never' if your life has been touched by God! After she left school she went to stay with her parents in Vellore, and the happenings of one night were to change her life.

Early one evening an Indian came to the door of her doctor father's house. Ida saw at a glance that he was a high-caste Brahmin by his priestly dress.

'Can I do anything for you?' asked Ida.

'Oh yes, ammal, I desperately need your help.' The man went on to say that his wife, a girl of fourteen, was dying in childbirth, and please would Ida come and save her. Ida said that she was not the doctor, but that she would call her father. The young man was horrified. 'Take a *man* into my house to care for my wife?' He turned away with sadness, and went on his way.

Ida went back to her room, and while she was writing a letter there was another knock on her door. Excitedly she thought it was the Brahmin returning with a change of mind, but no, it was a strange man before her when she opened the door. He said that his wife was dying in childbirth, and he had heard that a doctor had come from America recently, and please would she come and attend his wife. Again Ida had to tell the man that the doctor was her father, and again the man refused to have a man attend his wife. 'Only the men of her immediate family ever enter a Muslim woman's apartment. It is you, a woman, who I want.' Ida explained that she had no medical knowledge. 'Then my wife must die. It is the will of Allah,' and the man left.

Ida returned to her room but by now she was too upset to continue writing her letter, instead she busied herself in her room. It was then that the third call came. When she opened the door she recognised the man as the father of one of her pupils at the Hindu girls' school. He was very distressed and said that his wife was seriously ill, and please would she come. Once more Ida explained the situation, and she could see his outraged dignity and the bitterness of his disappointment as he turned away.

It was then, when she was back in her room, that Ida experienced a direct call from God, to which she did not find easy to say yes. She was told that she should become a doctor and return to Vellore to minister to women in need. The next day she asked a servant to visit the three houses to find out how the women were. He returned and told her that all three women were dead. One does not require a great imagination to realise the powerful effect this had on Ida.

She went back to America, trained to be a doctor, qualified and returned to Vellore at the beginning of the century. She started her hospital with one bed, one nurse and herself. Today it is one of the great hospitals in the East: it has a training college for men and women to be doctors and a training college for women to be nurses; it does all the major surgery of the present day and it has private paying patients who help subsidise its costs, as the greater part of the hospital's work is done for free, or according to the ability of the patients to pay. It is a truly remarkable place, begun and carried through by a remarkable woman. She is Aunt Ida to thousands of grateful patients and qualified doctors and nurses who are now spread throughout the world.

Vellore was a fascinating place. I would borrow a bicycle and cycle into the town, but I had to be ready to jump off at a moment's notice in the case of a cow sauntering across the road, or because someone would cross the road without looking. The driver of a car or bus would keep his hand down on the horn to warn people, so there would be a cacophony of sound to mix with other sounds of buying and selling from the stalls along the way. The women I saw all seemed beautiful in their brilliantly coloured saris – what graceful garments they are. Their skin did not seem to age in the same way as the skin of women of the West, and their brown eyes were full of kindness.

And so the weeks flew by, and each day it seemed to me that Gwenda looked a little better. I think it would be true to say that having me there helped her, as we were able to laugh a lot together, and laughter is a wonderfully healing exercise. All too soon it was time for me to be thinking about my return to England. The first thing I had to do was send for my money, held in Aden by the agent. When it arrived and was changed into Indian rupees, it came to 1856 rupees and .08 annas. The hospital authorities saw to my travel bookings: train to Madras, plane to Colombo, and a ship from there to England. It was done through Thomas Cook, Ltd, and when I received the account it was for 1856 rupees and .08 annas! Really, I should have kept the proof of this; why I didn't I do not know. To me though, it is an acclamation that I had indeed been 'kept by the Power'.

There can be no doubt in my mind, as I look back over thirty-five years, that my acceptance of all the strange and wonderful things that happened to me during this saga was through my utter reliance and trust in God's overriding control. I cannot in any other way explain my blissful lack of concern throughout (with the exception of the day of my arrival at the Bombay Airport!) From the time the captain told me that the money could be refunded, of my acceptance that I would have to leave the ship and fend for myself, my willingness to leave a large amount of money with a complete stranger, with only his visiting card to say he had it, my utter lack of concern or planning while I was flying through the air to Bombay, my acceptance of the wonderful way travel arrangements were made for me without my knowledge, the planning that was done for me for my return to England, culminating in this extraordinary money phenomenon, it all seemed so right!

Saying goodbye was a difficult time for Gwenda and me. It had meant a lot to Gwenda to have one of the family with her at such a traumatic time. For me, it was bad enough to see the sister I loved so helpless, but to know that I was going too far away to visit her again or to watch her as she started to recover was not easy. Her courage and her acceptance of this crippling disease had caught the imagination and admiration of all who saw her, and I was very proud to be her sister. I will never forget two things she said to me at that time. One was: 'If I had to have an illness I am grateful that it is not a painful one,' and another time she said, 'Of course I am praying that I will be healed, but if I can witness to God better from a wheelchair, then I will accept that.'

And that was what did happen. Gwenda has never walked again, but there is no shadow of doubt that she has been an inspiration and encouragement to all those whose lives she touched.

My return journey was comparatively uneventful. I flew from Madras to Colombo, where I was met by a Baptist missionary who gave me hospitality for the night and showed me around. There was very little time but my recollections are of a lovely city and surroundings. The next day I boarded a huge P&O liner and I was staggered by the size of it. I had a cabin to myself, with a door opening on to one of the decks. I liked that, and I can recall an amusing episode.

I have always been proud of the fact that I am a good sailor. There had been a storm at sea when we were going through the Bay of Biscay aboard the *Warwick Castle*. The Bay of Biscay is notorious for storms and it certainly lived up to its reputation. I felt proud of myself when at the height of this storm dinner was announced and I went down to the dining hall only to find I was one of the very few. We all sat at the captain's table. I enjoyed that meal and felt most smug!

So you can imagine my horror and dismay when I started to feel sick when this monster of a liner ran into bad weather. I was furious and I can see myself now, going onto the deck, leaning over the side and telling myself, 'You will *not* be sick! Glenys, you will *not* be sick!' And I wasn't. To make quite sure, I went down to my cabin, put a deckchair outside my cabin door and wrapped myself in a rug determined to sit it out. I triumphed.

Unlike my voyage as far as Aden, on which I loved every moment, my voyage home holds few memories for me. The ship was too big to allow that lovely feeling of being a close-knit group, doing things together and enjoying one anothers' company. This time I seemed to have to walk miles to get anywhere, and I was always meeting strangers.

One recollection I do have is of a time when I sat at a big table in the dining salon, and three people there tried to chum up with me: a husband and wife, and another man. They were returning after a working visit to Australia, where they seemed to have made a lot of money which they were spending with gay abandon, even to the point of drinking Drambuie before breakfast. I have never drunk Drambuie since!

One evening after dinner they suggested we should go to my cabin for a chat and a drink. Even then I was very naive and I agreed to this. Later the husband and wife got up and left the man in the cabin with me. I was furious! I must be quite intimidating when angry, because he certainly left with his tail between his legs! We did not have much contact after that.

Why was I so angry? It wasn't just that I thought the husband and wife were taking things for granted in assuming I wanted to be left alone with their friend. I have no doubt it had been planned between the three of them. But it was more than that. I think I have always been out of my depth when men have made sexual advances to me. I haven't known how to behave, so fear has entered into my behaviour, leading to a fierce anger. Somewhere I have read that if a young girl is unable to form natural patterns of behaviour with boys, then in adult life she is unlikely to form a natural relationship with a man and will often have unrewarding, unsatisfactory relationships with married men. That has been my experience twice in my life. (Not that I ever went 'the whole hog' as we said in my day – I was far too inhibited for that.)

Looking back, I find it rather bewildering that I cannot recall *at all* what happened when I arrived at Tilbury Docks, London. The experience had shaken me more than I realised.

CHAPTER TEN

New Zealand Beckons

In my tenth year as head deaconess of the Guildford Diocese, early in 1959, Pam Rhodes spent twenty-four hours with me. It was during this time that she told me the senior Anglican chaplain of the hospitals in Christchurch, New Zealand, was looking for a woman to help him in his work. Pam said that it would be just the right job for me, as a state registered nurse and a deaconess of the church. I was 'just right.' She was sure I would get on well with Sam as he was 'a dear.' I was astounded at the thought of going to New Zealand. Nothing would make me do that. I didn't even know where it was!

Pam insisted that she write to Sam Woods about me, and I told her she could write to Sam as often as she liked but no way would I go to New Zealand! Yet in my long life I have discovered that it is a great mistake to say no like that. I had committed my life to God, and I could expect surprises. The Creator of the Universe must have a wonderful sense of humour.

Pam did write, and Sam wrote back to me saying that he was really keen for me to join him, but first he would have to ask the Christchurch diocesan standing committee to finance the venture. Later he wrote to say that the standing committee would not even consider it. It was quite out of the question to pay money to a project that would involve bringing a woman out from Britain, paying the fare and the stipend. There had never been a woman as a full-time hospital chaplain before. It was quite a preposterous idea!

That settles it, I thought, and went on with my life in Guildford. But some months later I heard from Sam again. He had decided to try to raise the money privately and he succeeded in getting enough for my voyage to New

Zealand by ship, and to pay my stipend for three months. I accepted the challenge.

Pam had told me that a car would be essential, but I was unable to think of buying one with the proverbial sixpence in the bank. But the Lord moves in mysterious ways. My dear friend Helen Douglas, who had raised the money for my cruise, had recently died. In her will she had left me £300 sterling, which was enough to buy a new car. Her sister Mary paid for it to be transported to New Zealand. I think it was this unexpected gift, coming when it did, that convinced me it was right for me to accept and go to New Zealand. I left England in November 1959, spent Christmas with Gwenda in Vellore, and arrived in New Zealand on 1 January 1960. Kept by the Power? (Sadly, Pam Rhodes died in South Africa of cancer of the lymphatic system within two days of my arrival.)

My last weeks in England were a very difficult and emotional time for me, and there is almost a complete blank in my mind of that period. I must have gone to Wales to say my farewells to my sister Enid and the folks there, to Russington to say goodbye to my sister Jean and her family, and then throughout the diocese of Guildford where I had spent the last ten years, but I can recall none of it. However, I do remember that I insisted that there should be no-one to see me off from the Tilbury Docks, and I can recall that during the voyage I bought a pair of cherry-coloured slacks, something I had never worn in England. Had I even then discarded the prim and proper behaviour of a deaconess in England in the expectation of a freer life in New Zealand? I do not know. I know of no more except for a snapshot I have of me sitting on deck smoking a cigarette with a woman friend.

I left the ship at Colombo, Ceylon (now Sri Lanka), and was met by a friend of Gwenda's who looked after me until I flew to India to

Head deaconess at Guilford.

spend Christmas with Gwenda. It was wonderful to see my sister back in harness as senior anaesthetist in Vellore Hospital, after her serious bout of polio.

After Christmas I flew back to Ceylon to meet up with another ship, and was once again under way to my new life. The ship was due to arrive at Wellington, and Sam had said that he would meet me there and escort me on the ferry to Christchurch. The exciting day arrived, and as the great ship moored I hung over the rails looking at the people below who had come to meet their friends. I could see three 'dog-collars,' and as I looked at the three men my heart sank: I did not think much of any of them from where I was standing. But, to my amazement, the three gathered their friends and left the wharf and I was left hanging over the ship's rails with no-one left below to meet me!

When I had collected my wits, I went down to the purser and told him my story, and he phoned the archdeacon in Christchurch to find out what had happened. Dear Sam: he had got the dates mixed and was happily sitting in Christchurch – but when he found out he was not so happy. He gave the purser the phone number of a friend of his to ask him to look after me for the day and see me on the ferry at 8pm. The kind friend obliged. I was to meet him in half an hour in a certain hotel and was drinking tea when he arrived. He had to go to work but said that his wife would collect me around noon. Feeling safe again, I explored what I could of Wellington and had my hair shampooed and set.

The charming wife arrived and took me to their home with a beautiful view and looked after me until it was time to catch the night ferry to Christchurch.

I was very grateful to these friends of Sam's and soon settled in for the night in my single cabin and slept well. I was up very early as we docked around 7am at Lyttelton, and I wanted to see what I was coming to. I think I fell in love with New Zealand then and there. It was all so beautiful: the morning light, the clear sea, the cliffs of Banks Peninsula and the harbour itself with its many bays. This time when we docked there was great excitement around me – even the dog came on board with Sam and two others of his family. I remember we laughed a lot over Sam's default, and I immediately knew that here was a family I would love and be happy with. What a glorious relief!

Back in their home we had breakfast together, seven of us. I felt very much at home and the eldest son, Richard, went into the kitchen and said, 'Mum! She's neat!' High praise indeed!

Thanks to Helen from my Guildford days, I had my own car, the first car that I had owned. What a joy, as I have always been a bit crazy about cars and driving. The first thing I did was to go seeking a furnished flat. Mary, Helen's sister (my benefactor), had arranged that she would send me half the cost of renting a flat. Her words to me were that it was important that I should have comfortable quarters to live in when I was so far away from my home and friends. She also gave me a further £300 so that I could return to England if I couldn't settle in New Zealand. It was so wonderful.

So I went flat-hunting. I found a place I thought was just right and went back to Sybil, Sam's wife, and told her with great pride that I had just found my new flat, with a sunroom facing south to catch the sun. Sybil started to chuckle and said, 'Glenys, you do realise that you won't get any sun in your sunroom if it is facing south? The sun shines from the north down under.'

How right she was. However, I stayed in that flat for about six months and through my first winter. I couldn't believe that the sun could have such warmth in winter, and I would put on a coat and sit in the garden to eat my lunch rather than sit in my cold sunroom. On my day off I would pack a lunch and go to the slopes of the Port Hills, sit there on the grass, wearing a cardigan, enjoy my lunch and marvel at the warmth. I thought I had come to Utopia!

I loved my work as a hospital chaplain. Mind you, in 1960 I was not allowed to be called a chaplain, but an *assistant* to the chaplain. But that did not worry me as the work was so tremendously worthwhile. Working with Sam was a joy, and we had lots of fun and laughter, which was just as well as we had many sad and harrowing situations to cope with.

The lady superintendent, Mrs Chambers, took me under her wing and was especially kind to me when she found out I was a trained nurse and midwife. I was invited to the lunch and afternoon breaks for senior staff, which were held with her in a small sitting room. I enjoyed this as it helped me to get to know the senior staff. Mrs Chambers took me in her car to the foothills of the Southern Alps, where we walked and shared 'billy-can' tea, cooked on a wood fire. She had been a farmer's wife and I could tell how much she loved the wild places. Her husband had died quite young and she had trained as a nurse.

I found the work fascinating. Three times a week we would start the day early by taking the Reserved Sacrament (that is, Holy Communion) to the patients on the wards. The previous day we had found out who wanted to receive it. In those days we were only allowed to give the Sacrament to Anglicans, although our ward ministry was to all who were interested. Things have changed so much since then. Although I was an ordained deaconess I was not permitted to administer the Sacrament. So I would 'go before' Sam to the ward, gather the folk together, screen them off and then join them in the short service. I remember one of the staff nurses asking me if I minded having to do the menial tasks. I said, 'No, not really. I think of myself as a kind of John the Baptist, who "went before".' We smiled at each other as we passed on to do our work.

Many events stand out in my mind from that time, and I will relate two of them.

I was visiting on the women's orthopaedic ward and I went out onto the balcony where there were four beds. The patient in the third bed told me she had had an operation a week earlier and she had to go back to the operating theatre tomorrow for a few stitches inside. It was a minor job but she had convinced herself she was going to die. She was a Roman Catholic so I was able to talk with her, encourage her and pray with her. The next morning I was doing my rounds in different wards when at about 11am I had a strong urge to go to this ward and see how my friend was doing. She had had her operation and was out of the anaesthetic, but she looked ghastly. Her face was grey and her hand when I held it was cold and clammy. She whispered to me that she was going to die. In myself I agreed with her, but I told her not to be silly, that she was doing fine.

I went back into the ward and asked a staff nurse, who was changing a dressing, if she would please come and look at this patient. She did, and assured me that she was doing nicely. But I had a strong feeling, and my training told me that she would die if not attended to. So I went straight to the phone, and tracked down Mrs Chambers, who was doing her 'rounds'. I asked her to come straight away, telling her the patient was in shock and critically ill. The matter was not mentioned again, but when I went up to the ward later on I found she had been moved to the ward's critically ill area, and her bed was on 'shock-blocks.' The matter seemed to be closed and not so much as a thank-you came my way, but I realised that it was quite a sensitive situation. The staff nurse was a good nurse but she was busy and no doubt felt that I was interfering on her turf, so she didn't really look at her patient with 'seeing' eyes.

I remember that occasion vividly because it was one of many times I have

Chaplain at Christchurch Public Hospital, with Nurse Frances Hamilton (later Blakely).

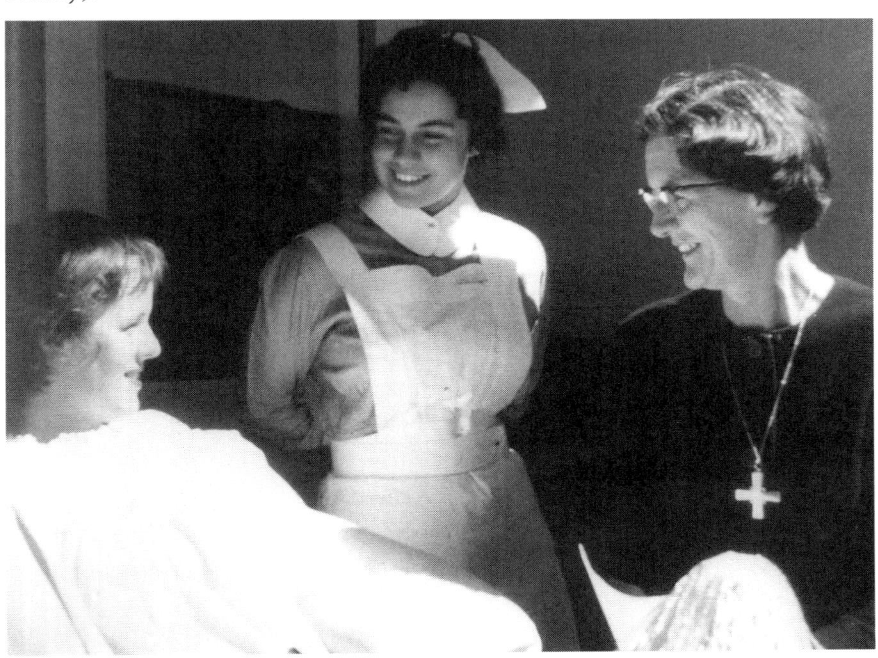

felt an inner compulsion to do something, to go somewhere and always that conviction has been right. To me it is the movement of God, who can do these things through anyone who is open and receptive to His energy. The woman recovered and we laughed together over her fears. She never knew of the drama played out for her by others.

I found that one had to be sensitive and flexible with the patients. One moment I could be laughing and joking with a group of patients and the next moment move into the deep waters of a patient's needs. I remember one day I went onto the balcony of a men's ward to find a group were playing darts. I watched them for a while and then said, 'You chaps don't know how to play that game; you are supposed to hit that little spot in the centre!'

The reply came back in a flash, 'Okay, Deaconess, you show us how to do it!'

'Certainly!' I said. 'No problem,' and I took a dart in my hand. Now, I had never actually thrown a dart before, but away it went, and – bullseye! Imagine it! How we laughed, and one of the men said, 'Do it again!' to which I quickly replied, 'Not on your life!' It made their day and mine.

I went back into the ward and the very next patient was needing all the love, understanding and encouragement of God that I had within me to give him. And so it went on day after day and week after week: such a mixture of fortitude and resignation, of pain and stoicism, of tears and laughter, and always their need for me to be with them to share their present mood.

In those days a ward could hold up to thirty patients, and I recall one instance when all of them who could be were convulsed in laughter. I had been talking to an elderly man at the top of the ward. He called himself an atheist and we were enjoying quite a lengthy discussion when I started to move down the ward. He kept on talking to me so that I had to stop and reply, until I got to the end of the ward. By this time he was shouting at me and I did likewise. The men loved it as it was all done in good part, neither side winning!

I remember preparing one young man, a long-stay patient for confirmation. The great day arrived and the bishop came to take the service. Bishop A.K. Warren was a fine figure of a man and I can see him now, dressed in all his ecclesiastical glory – cope, mitre and all sweeping down the main corridor with his robes fanning out behind him. It really did make folk sit up and take notice, and I guess the young man never forgot that occasion.

Our lovely chapel was in constant use. We chaplains had our vestry/office there; we held individual services, or sat chatting together, and the Nurses' Christian Fellowship met there. Every Sunday there would be a service to which patients would come on foot or in their beds. There was a roster of young people from nearby churches who would come to help the orderlies push the beds or wheelchairs down the long corridors, and those nursing staff who could come, would come along too.

Thirty years after I left the hospital I am still in touch with three of the nurses from the fellowship. All three are married. One lives in Australia, one in the North Island and the third lives on the West Coast, where she is now an Anglican priest and vicar of her church. I value those contacts.

Sadly, with the rebuilding of the hospital, the chapel became redundant. It was saved from demolition but not without a fight. It is now a historic treasure and the only monument in New Zealand to the nurses who fought and gave their lives in World War II.

Despite the marathon effort of travelling throughout New Zealand to put the Ministry of Women in the Church 'on the map,' the most satisfying, enjoyable and worthwhile work I have ever undertaken in the church has been the two and a half years I spent as a chaplain at Christchurch Hospital. I made many friends and was given a wonderful welcome to my new land. I loved this country from the moment I arrived at Lyttelton and became a New Zealand citizen in 1974.

CHAPTER ELEVEN

On the Road for Women!

Early in 1962 the Christchurch Council for Women's Church Work was trying to find ways to recruit women to the Order of Deaconesses and to start a house for their training. The council felt that only the establishment of such a provincial training house would further the work of women in the church, but the Christchurch Diocese lacked the resources to fund such training. The council members believed that if all seven dioceses in New Zealand could be made aware of the advantages of this form of women's ministry, then the church of the province itself might be stirred into action.

But the majority of church people in New Zealand did not know that such an order existed, so how could women come forward for training? It was obvious that we needed someone to travel throughout the country to 'spread the good news.'

As in everything else, we needed money to do this, and permission from the bishops of the seven dioceses. It was decided to apply straight to the Christchurch Synod for a grant. To support the council's cause I was invited to address the synod in October 1962, the first time a woman would address synod 'from the floor'.

Understandably I was pretty nervous, so after I had written my address, I asked one of the senior clergy to read it and give me the okay. He read it and pronounced it unusable! Synod was a legal body and it would be quite inappropriate to appeal to the 'emotions' of members, he said. I thanked him for his opinion.

The day came. I was not permitted to sit on the floor of 'the House' but was relegated to the gallery with the onlookers. When my time came, I entered the

House and stood facing the male-dominated synod. On the platform were the Bishop in his robes, the legal 'bod' in his gown and wig, both looking very forbidding. Altogether it was rather awesome. All I could do was face the bishop and say, 'My lord, I find myself in a dilemma. I took my address to a senior member of the clergy for his opinion and I was told that no way could I say what I had prepared, because synod is a legal body and I was proposing to appeal to members' emotions. The trouble is, my lord, that I am about to do just that!'

The House erupted into gales of laughter, and I had them in the palm of my hand. I have found over and over again, that if one can introduce lightness, laughter and a touch of fun into public speaking it draws you closer to your audience. The council was given a grant sufficient for the work to go ahead.

Next was to seek the permission of the seven diocesan bishops for a representative to travel throughout each diocese to spread the 'good news' that there was an ordained ministry for women, the Order of Deaconesses, in the Anglican Church in New Zealand. Only Christchurch and Waiapu were so far aware of its existence.

The council asked me if I would be that representative and take on the arduous task of travelling alone, by car, throughout New Zealand, to meet and speak to thousands of people in a period over eighteen months. I leapt at it and accepted it as another 'push from God.' As I moither over what I'm writing, I am again amazed at the way my life was taken over. Not once after my work in the London parish did I apply for a job; I felt that I was 'put' there in each case, and it gave me a wonderful feeling of security, that each job was where I should be.

The Bishop of Christchurch was keen on the project to go ahead, so that was one bishop on our side. During my holiday in February 1963 I visited the six other bishops and found them all willing also. I recall one enjoyable instance of that time. Because I was doing this travel in my holiday I wore 'mufti' – no stockings, sandals, and a sleeveless dress instead of my deaconess garb. In Nelson I was on my way to see Bishop Hulme-Moir and I stopped outside a drive entrance of what I thought could be Bishopscourt. There was a lodge beside the gates and a man dressed in a khaki shirt and shorts working in the garden. I said to him, 'Please, is this the bishop's house?'

The man said, 'Yes, who do you want to see?'

'I've come to see the Bishop', I replied.

'Well, I'm the bishop, and who might you be?'

'I'm that deaconess whom you are expecting to stay the night.'

'Great Scott!' exclaimed he.

'Crumbs!' said I, and we both dissolved into laughter. From then on we were friends. He was a lovely man.

I was not commissioned by the Bishop of Christchurch for this venture until May. There were two problems facing me: one was my flat and the other was my car. The Morris Oxford I had brought from England was not quite long enough for my long legs, so I had difficulty on a long-distance drive. So how would I motor the length and breadth New Zealand? I could not do all that travelling in my car, and no way would I get money for a car out of the diocese. In the end I decided to use the £300 that had been given to me before I left England (my homesick money), sold my car and bought myself a Vauxhall Victor, which became my best friend.

The second problem was wonderfully answered for me by the Vicar of St Michael's in Christchurch. He had retired and was going to England for at least a year, and he offered me his cottage in Diamond Harbour, rent free. Perfect. I could go to a diocese for a month or so, then come back and relax and recover in 'my' cottage in Diamond Harbour.

Without that time and space between each diocese, I doubt whether I would have been able to finish the job. It was massive. For the next eighteen months I travelled the country from Hokianga in the north to Bluff in the south. I addressed four of the seven synods, preached in five of the cathedrals, addressed over 300 meetings and spoke to over 22,000 people.

Along the way an interesting debate arose, and of all the work in the church I was required to do, I think my involvement in this was my most significant contribution. The previous General Synod had formed a committee to prepare a 'Form and Manner of Making of Deaconesses,' based on the English form, which had been used in New Zealand for years, and to bring it to the General Synod in 1964. The chairman of this committee was a

Christchurch archdeacon and shortly before the 1964 General Synod he showed the committee's efforts to another archdeacon and myself. We were appalled. They had removed from the form every mention of the word 'ordination,' which is a word of key importance as it means that a deaconess is within the ordained ministry of the church. This word is used frequently in the English form and its removal from the proposed New Zealand form represented a significant 'downgrading' of the deaconess's role.

The Christchurch deaconesses were very disturbed and time was against us – we had to think fast. Fortunately, I awoke one morning with a brainwave. We would produce a sheet setting out the two forms side by side, and produce enough copies to put before the members of synod (see Appendix III). The Dean kindly said that he would speak to it, and I was told to go to Auckland to attend the synod myself. It was a wonderful experience. The committee's proposed 'Form and Manner…' was thrown out at the first sitting and the archbishop formed a small committee to devise an alternative.

The committee spent half the night forming a new one; a student stayed up to cyclostyle enough copies to bring to synod the next day. The new form, with the word 'ordained' reinstated where necessary, was passed without challenge. During the break several of the synodsmen came up and congratulated me. I was only a spectator but it gave me a warm feeling of acceptance. I believe that the role I was able to perform in the granting of canonical status to the Order of Deaconesses was a crucial one for women's ministry. It is not too much to say that the ordination of women first to the diaconate and soon after to the priesthood, might well have been diverted down another path, perhaps for a number of years, if it had not been for this interesting happening.

I continued my travels, and recorded my experiences in two logbooks, which have been lodged in the archives at St John's Theological College in Auckland. Anyone interested should be able to look at these without my boring you here. However, it was such a high point of my life that I will relate some of the highlights here.

The logbook reads that on Monday 17 June 1963 I 'Left Christchurch at 11.15 am on my first tour of this great venture. May our dear Lord be my strength, my guide, my wisdom, my concern and compassion, my inspiration.

Lord Jesus, this is Your Life – to do with as You will.' And I set out.

I was in the vestry of Wellington Cathedral one Sunday as I was to be the preacher. The bishop, dean and the curate were there with me and the dean asked the bishop, 'Where shall I put the deaconess to sit? Shall I put her in the sanctuary?'

The Bishop had a very English voice, and he drawled his reply: 'Well, I don't think so. When I was a vicar in England I always distinguished between the deaconess and the clergy.' He said this in front of me, and the way he said it made me steaming mad. The dean went out and when he returned he said to the bishop, 'I think I have that sorted out.' I thought I detected a twinkle in his eye and I soon knew why. The dean had put a chair for me directly opposite the Bishop's throne!

I was still pretty shaken as I went into the pulpit, by the way the bishop had belittled the Order of Deaconesses, so in my address I emphasised that a deaconess was an ordained woman; that she was part of an ancient order going back to the fourteenth century when Bishop Chrysostom had a permanent Ordained Order of Deacons for both men and women. After I had said that, I stopped and held the silence for a moment, then said in a clipped clear voice, 'Is that quite clear?' I looked across at the curate and he winked at me.

After the service my knees were like jelly as I was to dine with the bishop! But he was delightful and I like to think that he enjoyed it. I always faced these challenges head-on throughout my tour, and it seemed to work.

In another diocese the bishop asked one of his archdeacons to have me for the weekend in his parish and arrange for me to preach on Sunday and talk to groups where possible. The archdeacon clearly didn't want me – he didn't want me to preach in his church or to stay in his home – but he couldn't refuse. I knew of this so you can imagine I wasn't exactly looking forward to my weekend. I can recall delaying my arrival at the vicarage on the Saturday for as long as possible. I went down to the sea and ate a sandwich lunch in the car, while a seagull sat on the bonnet watching every mouthful.

When I arrived at the vicarage I was given a cool reception and told that at 5pm he was taking me to the Anglican secondary school for girls to speak to the boarders. When we got there he took me into a large room where the boarders were sitting on the floor watching television. The vicar went over to the TV, turned it off, then turned to the girls and said, 'I'm sorry to spoil your fun, but you have to listen to Deaconess Lewis talking to you.'

What an introduction! What was my response? I turned to the girls with my face alight with laughter. 'Phew what an introduction,' I said. 'I'm sure you cannot wait to hear me.' And we all burst into laughter and had a really enjoyable time together. The vicar thawed quite a bit after that. Next day I preached at the morning service, and we ended up being friends.

In yet another diocese I was asked again to speak to the girls of an Anglican high school. This time it was in the school chapel so I had to wear my official dress, which was a navy blue cassock and blue veil. Later during my stay in that diocese I was told that one of the younger girls who heard me in the chapel had gone home and told her mother, 'Mummy, what do you think? We had a dinosaur to speak to us this morning!' I did enjoy that!

During my time in Nelson I stayed with Bishop Hulme-Moir and his wife. One Sunday he was taking me to the cathedral to preach, and as he parked his car outside I saw the dean at the door dressed in a purple cassock. In those days purple was the prerogative of bishops, so I said, 'What is the dean doing dressed in purple?' He replied, 'Oh, he likes to.' I liked that, and the man who said it.

In yet another diocese there was again an upset as to where I was to sit. This I had to deal with myself, and I reminded the clergy that a deaconess was ordained, and should be seated with the clergy. This was done but after the service the dean said to me, 'Deaconess, don't forget you are only a very little person!' I was really amused, as he was a very short man, and I am a rather tall woman!

I stayed with a vicar and his family in the parish that included Opononi, famous for its friendly dolphin. He took me there for a Mothers' Union service in a small church in a field. The service was to begin at 2.30pm and we arrived at a meeting house where the women were preparing a hangi – eats for afterwards. The vicar was going over to the church to get things ready and I said I would go with him. It was by then about 2.30, but he said there was no hurry. As we walked over I was delighted to see two young girls running over the long grass towards the church carrying wild flowers for the service. I don't recall the time we finally started but I do recall the fun we had, in the church and afterwards as we shared a meal together. The group were mainly Maori and they paid me the compliment of saying that I was like one of them, to which I answered, 'It must be because I am Welsh!' Going back in the car afterwards the vicar said to me, 'You cannot know what a joy this afternoon has been. The archdeacon did a visitation recently and he told me that I should discipline my flock and not allow them to laugh in church.' Oh dear!

A typical day of my tour is this one in Wellington, recorded in my logbook. At 8am there was Holy Communion for the clergy of the archdeaconry, after which would be a meeting where I would give an address; on this occasion it was the Archdeaconry Clerical Association. I remember one of the clergy saying, 'I cannot understand why deaconesses lust after ordination.' How charming! (Of course what he really meant was 'lust after ordination to the priesthood,' as deaconesses are already ordained. I had refused to speak about the priesthood as I knew it would kill my mission if that notion reared its head.)

After this meeting, at 11am, I spoke to the Archdeaconry Mothers' Union, a nice warm group, and then it was on to the Belmont Archdeaconry Clerical Association, where I lunched with them and spoke as well. In the evening I spoke to the Khandallah Mothers' Union Evening Group. My logbook records that I addressed 125 people that day, and it ends: 'Quite a day.'

Another extract from the Auckland Diocese records shows that it wasn't always easy. At a synodial service at 8am the clergy were robed and I felt completely overcome by the solid phalanx of men and wondered what in the world I was doing there. My task suddenly seemed impossible and I felt so alone and isolated. Panic continued most of the day as I tried to prepare what I was going to say to synod the next day. Every draft I tore up and felt dreadful.

However, I spoke to synod for 20 minutes and was given a warm reception. One of the clergy who had been at the Christchurch Synod when I spoke there said that I was better than ever, but I lost my voice in the evening.

Another time I was invited by the warden, Dr John Foster, to spend the day at St John's Theological College, to speak to the staff, students and staff wives, and to have dinner in the refectory. At dinner the warden sat me at his right hand at high table and during the meal he said, 'Do you know, Deaconess, that you are the first woman to sit for a meal in this refectory?' Another first: the first woman to address a synod; the first woman to occupy a pulpit in several cathedrals; and now the first woman to sit at high table. Goodness!

While I was in the Dunedin Diocese, I had to fly to the Waiapu Synod in Napier, then back to Dunedin in twenty-four hours to speak to the Dunedin Synod next day. I was also interviewed by newspaper and magazine journalists and spoke on radio, so bringing to the wider public the opportunities open to women for work in the church.

My last day on tour started with 7am Holy Communion at Hamilton Cathedral, after which I motored to Paeroa for the 9.30am morning service. On the way I was exhausted and felt quite unable to cope with what I had to do. I prayed and was wonderfully carried through and the vicar told me afterwards that he didn't know when he had heard a sermon that had moved and inspired him so much. I told him that it wasn't me and explained my exhaustion before the service. I thanked God for this and the many other blessings and for upholding me so wonderfully over the whole tour.

However, I wasn't quite finished. I went on to Hikutaia to another Holy Communion service, where I was able to rest on a bed after lunch at the vicarage, before going on to Cambridge. The vicar and his wife were very kind and after tea we went to Evensong. It was a friendly service with many generous remarks at the end. Altogether it was a lovely day for my last speaking engagements. I left Cambridge at 8.40pm and arrived at the Lakeside Lodge at Taupo at 10.30 and settled in for the night. On Monday I motored to Wellington and on Wednesday, after 23,600 miles, I arrived at Diamond Harbour and home. I had spoken at 305 public meetings.

At this point I would like to share a prayer much used at the time:

> My God, I desire to love You perfectly:
> With all my heart which You made for Yourself;
> With all my mind which only You can satisfy;
> With all my soul which fain would soar to You;

With all my strength, my feeble strength which
        shrinks before so great a task, and yet can do
        nought else but spend itself in loving You.
Claim my heart;
Fill my mind;
Uplift my soul and
Reinforce my strength
That where I fail You may succeed in me,
And make me love You perfectly.

– Author unknown

My car was my best friend during those months. It was taxing moving into the houses of strangers each night. While they were really kind to me it was nevertheless a strain all the time. The only time I could relax was when I was alone in my car, and it was very restful. I would pull into the side of the road to eat a lunch or to have a sleep. I would sing or talk to myself. Despite two broken windscreens and four punctures, my car was still my best friend!

I did know that the Bishop of Auckland, after the time I had spent in his diocese when on tour, was keen to open a deaconess training house and wanted me to run it. But first he had to get funding from the diocese. As usual, no way was the standing committee of the diocese going to produce money to open, furnish and run a training house for deaconesses. But once again the bishop succeeded in gathering the money privately. He planned to use Selwyn House, an old historic house in Parnell, for this purpose.

Three events in my life, relating to the need for funds for work I was to do, have given me a great sense of being affirmed by God, who moves in such mysterious ways and has such a lively sense of humour! Fancy me getting the better of the members of three standing committees! I also felt affirmed by the people who put their trust in me.

The following year, 1965, I visited Britain for a much-needed holiday. My whole family were on the move that year. Jean and her family were on the high seas bound for Australia, where they have lived ever since. Jean has a large family now and is a great-grandmother. Gwenda was leaving Vellore Hospital, which was a sadness to her as her heart was in India. But she was still badly disabled and needed to earn some good money for her retirement. She was searching for work in Australia or New Zealand where the climate was kinder. We spent a lot of time together and I remember clearly a conversation we had during a picnic lunch in a field en route somewhere. Gwenda said, 'I have had a letter from the head anaesthetist at Christchurch Hospital in New Zealand offering me a position as senior anaesthetist, but I intend to turn it down as I think it will be warmer in Australia. What do you think?'

'That's a good one,' I said, 'Didn't you tell me that you would leave the decision in the Lord's hands? And here you are, turning down the first opening you have had!' Gwenda agreed with me: she shouldn't turn it down without exploring it. Mind you, I had a lot at stake, too. I badly wanted Gwenda in New Zealand with me.

So she accepted the position and came to Christchurch in 1965. We built two adjoining homes which we loved, nestled below the Port Hills. I was in Auckland at that time and didn't occupy mine until I retired in 1971. We were great buddies until she died on 13 February 1994.

During 1965 I received a formal invitation from the Bishop of Auckland to return to the Auckland Diocese as Head Deaconess and warden of the proposed new Deaconess House. This dual appointment involved preparing the historic house in Parnell for occupation, preparing the curriculum and timetable of study, interviewing students, conducting lectures at Deaconess House, and fulfilling other speaking and preaching engagements in the diocese. I took the job.

I organised field work and many other opportunities for the students to experience a wide variety of church work. Many visitors passed through Deaconess House in its first year, including Lady Fergusson, wife of the Governor-General, the archbishop and six other New Zealand bishops, and a variety of visitors from all over the world.

By April 1966 I had organised an association of Friends of Deaconess House Chapel, who received newsletters about the life and work of Deaconess House, contributing in return money, gifts and prayer support.

Financial management was another responsibility. In this I worked closely with the treasurer of the Board of Management and in 1967 managed to run the house on a budget of £1250! During my four-year term in this position, the work and training of deaconesses was continually publicised through the media. Throughout these years, and particularly during 1968-69, the status of women's work in the Anglican Church, and in the negotiating churches, evolved rapidly towards the priesthood. My work as warden of Deaconess House ended in December 1969, when women were accepted as full-time residential students at St John's Theological College, hitherto for men only.

From January 1970 to December 1971 I became warden of the Deaconess Centre and Hostel of the Holy Name in Auckland. This position involved management of a hostel for twenty-four tertiary women students, which I carried out without live-in paid staff. Deaconess visitors from overseas came to stay occasionally and retreats and seminars were held at the centre for both lay and ordained women, most of whom valued the beauty of the chapel and the opportunity for quiet reflection.

The four sisters in 1978. From left: Gwenda, Jean, Enid and Glenys.

At the age of sixty, at the end of 1971, I retired from my position as head deaconess, and shared a flat in Auckland for eighteen months with Aline Pengelly, my very good friend who has helped me so much with getting this book off the ground. But Aline was keen to go to Palmerston North to finish her degree, and I was wanting to live in my own home, so in 1973 I returned to Christchurch to live next door to Gwenda. By this time my eldest sister, Enid, was living with Gwenda. You will recall that Enid had polio when she was in her teens, but, unlike Gwenda who had to use a wheelchair, Enid was able to walk.

Enid had lived in Cardiff until she retired when she decided to come to New Zealand, live with Gwenda and be her 'housekeeper' as Gwenda was living a very full life as a senior anaethestist in the Christchurch hospitals. But it didn't work out and Enid bought her own flat near to us, and it worked happily. When Jean would visit us from Adelaide, the four of us would have much fun enjoying Gwenda's pool.

Enid died in 1988, peacefully and without pain. Gwenda developed post-polio syndrome some years later, which meant her muscles deteriorated again and she died of this in 1994. This leaves just Jean and me – one in Australia and the other in New Zealand – bad planning! Each of us goes, when we can, to see the other, and now it's my turn and a week from today I will arrive in Adelaide to visit her and Clive and her family, all of whom are loved.

I found that returning to Christchurch allowed some much-needed recovery for the next few years. The time in the Auckland Diocese had been strenuous and demanding, physically, mentally and emotionally.

The crowning moment came for me when, at the Auckland Synod of 1970, I was invited to second the motion: 'That this synod approves in principle the ordination of women to the priesthood.' That action represented for me what I call a complete mental somersault. I had moved from a vision of a permanent diaconate for men and women to a position where I found that I could say to the synod: 'I believe it is within the will and purpose of Almighty God that women should be ordained to the priesthood.

And so it was to be.

After seven years in retirement I was ordained a priest along with several

other women deacons in Auckland and in Christchurch. This meant returning to work, since you cannot be ordained in a vacuum – you have to receive
at the same time a licence to work. So I worked again for about two years
and loved it. There was a fullness and completeness about working as a priest
that was a very real experience. I worked in a relieving capacity: filling the
place of a vicar away on 'holiday' leave; returning to my great love hospital
chaplaincy; taking funerals, weddings and preaching.

As I write this in 1998 I am again retired and have just seen my eighty-
seventh birthday… enough is enough.

Glenys at work and at play.

Epilogue

During my long life I have had quite a few wonderful experiences and the following, for me, is one I will never forget.

In 1989 I married a delightful couple, both in their sixties. Both had grown-up children. Some months later Marg phoned me in great distress. Her daughter, who had been her lady-in-waiting at her wedding, had committed suicide. She was a lovely woman in her late thirties/early forties with three teenage sons. Marg asked me if I would take the funeral service at 11.15 on Wednesday. I said yes and carefully set about preparing myself for what I knew would be a difficult task.

On Wednesday morning I arrived at the crematorium a few minutes before eleven and found a large funeral already taking place. I parked at the entrance and waited in my car for the place to clear but it didn't. Puzzled, I thought I'd better explore, only to find that there was no 11.15 funeral booked. The director suggested it must be at the Harewood Crematorium, which was about twenty minutes away by car. It was by now 11 o'clock.

My mind went blank. I was in a state of shock. Another man came up and between them they tried to direct me to Harewood but I couldn't take it in. I had never been there; all the funerals I had taken had been at Linwood and I was hardly aware that there was another crematorium.

'Stop!' I cried. 'I can't take in a word you are saying!'

So the director said, 'I think the best thing is to get you a taxi.'

'Oh, great,' I said, 'I haven't any money.'

He replied: 'We will give you the money and I will phone the crematorium and tell them you have been delayed.' So I went to my car, collected my robes, got into the taxi and off we went.

The driver said, 'You want to get there by 11.15?' to which I replied, 'I have to get there, I'm taking the funeral!' So off we went like a bolt of lightning. He said, 'I hope you don't mind us breaking the speed limit?' to which I replied, 'Mind? I love it. Carry on as fast as you like.'

My mind was totally blank so we talked about how he was faring now that the taxi business had been deregulated, while he dodged through side ways and byways to avoid traffic lights. We got to the Crematorium in fifteen minutes!

To my astonishment there was standing room only. The chapel was full and the vestibule was overflowing. I went into the office to robe and the director came in and asked me if I wanted anything. 'Yes, a glass of water please.' Still my mind was a blank. I couldn't think of a thing! He came back and said that I still had a few minutes. Soon the pall-bearers began carrying the coffin into the chapel and everybody stood. I proceeded to walk through this mass of people. It was like walking through a forest with trees either side of me and still I couldn't think.

When I got to the front where Marg and her husband were standing I put my hand on Marg's hand and whispered, 'I'm sorry.' Jim, her husband, told me afterwards that my hands were shaking and he thought to himself: how in the world is Glenys going to manage?

I stepped onto the dais, put my books on the lectern and opened the service book to the right page. Then I looked up at the mass of people and suddenly it was as if I was "taken over". I was as cool, calm and collected as I have ever been in public speaking. I didn't make one single mistake. I spoke quietly and authoritatively, said what I had prepared to say. I did everything just as it should have been done, with complete serenity and calmness.

Afterwards I was overwhelmed by the number of people who came up to thank me and say how wonderful it had been, and how I had helped them by what I had said to come to terms with the tragedy they faced.

I wanted to shout out, 'It wasn't me! It wasn't me! I was "kept by the Power".' I had been empowered because I was in such a degree of shock that I couldn't think. I wanted to shout that out for everyone to hear.

When we were in the house afterwards a man came up to me and said, 'Normally when I am listening to a sermon or any public speaker my mind is busy thinking of all the things I want to do and am going to do, but this afternoon I was just rapt. I did not miss one word you said.' I just said, 'It wasn't me'.

Ray, Marg's son, came to my house later and said the same kind of thing. He said, 'A light shone from you.' That light wasn't me; I was empowered.

Jesus Said

Jesus said:
'Not one sparrow falls to the ground without your Father's consent. As for you, even the hairs of your head have all been counted.'

Lord, these words of Yours demand great faith in us today. Two thousand years ago the world was thought of as a house...

heaven in the attic,

hell in the basement,

the world between

But today Lord, we know of the cosmic universe – of galaxies, billions of light years away – whatever that means!

We know that there are worlds within worlds within the smallest atom.

We know that our bodies are composed of atoms that are constantly changing and being renewed.

We know that the cosmonauts have broken into this cosmos and have not found You – *Out There!*

You have promised us that not only are we known to You but that the very hairs of our head are numbered.

Not Easy to Believe.

It is not surprising, Lord, that there is among men today a seeking, searching, groping...

Longing for a belief in something: some being greater than the God taught in our Christian churches where the tendency is to put you in a box.

Child of My heart, take heart, there is still so much that you do not know or see. Where shall I begin?

What about the air you breathe? You cannot see it, feel it, touch it, yet it is pretty solid. Do you recall before the sound barrier was broken an aeroplane going beyond a certain speed would disintegrate, fall to pieces to the ground because the air had built up into a solid mass before it?

The writer of the Book of Wisdom knew this…

'When an arrow is shot, the air is parted and instantly closes up again and no-one can tell where it passed through.'

Or again:

The atom is so small that it cannot be seen with the naked eye; nor can My Cosmos in its entirety be seen by any of you on your tiny planet – clever though you are.

It does my heart good to see you searching, seeking, learning fresh truths about My universe.

You journey well and you journey far…

But My heart yearns for more of you to take the *Inward Journey*

It is hard but infinitely rewarding once you have committed yourself to this journey with Me.

Vistas will open up…

Not only of the you and Me within. This inward journey takes you out and glimpses of the cosmos appear. Don't expect to find Me in this experience overnight but, believe Me, it is the truth: each tiny fragment is essential to the whole. That is why even the hairs of your head are counted.

Are you still finding it too hard to swallow?

Let Me tell you why I came to earth 2000 years ago. The Bible says that I came in the fullness of time and that was right. I needed to demonstrate in a tangible human form the reality of God and Our love for you.

How else could We do it than by one of Us coming to show you? And this had to be done before man discovered the vastness of the Cosmos otherwise to believe in such love would be beyond the capacity of mankind…

and so I came…

I showed you beyond all reasonable doubt that God loves you, that love is costly, that pain is redemptive, and that no experience is lost or wasted.

So many things to tell you, to show you, so for the love you bear Me continue the journey inward.

APPENDIX I

Radio Transcripts

In recent years I have given a number of talks on radio, for the programmes *Comment* and *Soundings*. Here follow transcripts of some of those talks.

Coastal Shipping

Parliament works extra hours over the proposed open-coast shipping policy. But I would like to know if this extra work really shows a concern for our coastline and people.

Who knows? An ordinary citizen like myself may be forgiven for thinking this is one more straw in the wind, revealing a lack of protective caring for this land of ours.

I am a British citizen and also a citizen of my adoptive country, New Zealand. But, oh dear, these last few years have saddened me because I can see the writing on the wall.

Today Maori people are fighting, through the Waitangi Tribunal, to reclaim what is rightfully theirs of the land, rivers and coastline of New Zealand. If the present trend continues, tomorrow New Zealanders, Maori and Pakeha, will be fighting to reclaim their land, rivers and coast from foreign investment and occupation.

As I see it the British took over New Zealand by the sword and bloodshed. Today the takeover is happening again, not by the sword and bloodshed but silently, and in a more deadly way, by the mighty dollar.

I would like to know how many of our vital services still belong to New Zealanders. How much of our land has been sold, piecemeal, to overseas sources? To me this is the worst aspect. Once we lose our land we lose our country, as Maori know only too well.

Why is this allowed to go on? Does no-one care? What can an ordinary citizen do to stop this sell-out of our country? The answer is: I don't know!

My plea is: Put us in the picture. Spell out for us, clearly for all to see, what has already been sold, of our land and vital assets.

Dare I add: Before it is too late?

❧

Youth Suicide

I know a couple with five young children who lived on the Cashmere hills in Christchurch. They sold their property and moved to an old rambling house on the flat with a large wild garden of trees, shrubs and plenty of space for play. They have left the garden wild, put in a Para pool, tree-house and swings from tree branches. Because the garden is wild the children are free to play in it and to make their own fun. No TV or video games for them. And they are happy.

In the Christchurch *Press* I read of the 'Government Strategies to Cut Youth Suicide.' A group set up by the government in 1992 to study this tragic phenomenon released their report this month. It was produced by members of six government departments. The newspaper listed five of the recommendations. Two of them mentioned Maori and Pacific Island people but not one of them mentioned the need to look at family life and the lifestyle of the middle and upper grades in our society. Yet, a serious number of suicides come from that background. Why is there no study of suicides of this type of lifestyle? We see so many houses built on a postage-stamp piece of land so that the children are forced from their homes if they want to play outside.

Again in the *Press* of the 25 July I read an account of a unique Dunedin health survey to study 1000 young people from birth to adulthood and headed by Dr Phil Silva. It was stated that personality is formed during the first three years of life.

We all know the importance of the formative years of a child's life. Maybe the family I told you about know something of vital importance: that children need the security of the home; and space to develop their own fun and excitement, to enable them to be creative and resourceful in their own home space.

What happens to youngsters who in the material sense lack for nothing, yet have not been given the space to develop their own creative resources of mind and spirit? Is this their difficulty? So that when the stress and strain of adult life come along they have little within themselves to help them to cope?

It is good that the government has formed a group to study youth suicide. I think it would be even better if the group contacted Dr Silva to see what he can bring to the discussion.

Consumerism

There is a new fever attacking men, women and children throughout the Western world and spreading to Eastern countries. It is dangerous because it doesn't attack our physical bodies but it attacks our minds, and indeed, our whole way of life.

It is called consumerism, which makes it remote and not anything to do with us. So, let's bring it down to the nitty-gritty and call it Shopping Fever. This fever has spread at an alarming rate in recent years. No longer do we have the five-day working week for which our forebears fought so hard. This enabled families to live and play together, and even go to their baches for two whole days. We were given space.

Today, not only do we have a seven-day working week but, wait for it, at Christmas some stores are open all night. So real is the fever that people go to buy 'all thru' the night'.

This fever is being fed and nurtured by the policymakers of large complexes or stores. An example, when Sunday trading was introduced, the owner of a superstore decided not to open his store on Sunday, but soon after the store was open on Sunday like all the rest. It seems the owner of a small shop within a large complex is not allowed to decide when to open and to close. No, the owners of the complex make that decision. I asked the owner, 'What would happen if you decided to go your own way?'

The reply came back, 'I don't know. Anyone doing that would possibly be fined.'

What price freedom? Not only does this policy affect the owners, but also those who work in these places. They are afraid of losing their jobs if they don't agree to work the hours and days that used to be free.

Is this fever serious? Many would say that it is one of the reasons for the breakdown of the togetherness of family life. Mum and Dad and the kids are never all free at the same time.

But the fever is even deeper than that. Why do we use so much of our free time in shopping and spending? When and where did this fever begin and where will it take us?

Perhaps we need a group of sociologists to study this phenomenon. Once diagnosed, perhaps ways can be found to heal us of this new fever.

Losing Touch with God

My ways are not your ways – so says your God.

Thank goodness for that! You say the God you worship is the creator of the world and all that lives in it? You say he is all-powerful, all-seeing, and – the best joke of all – that he is all-loving.

You must be out of your mind to believe in such a God. Where is he/she now in the 1990s? Look around you and what do you see? Millions starving in different areas of the world. And what compounds the horror is the corruption, the black market, the sleek cars, the well-dressed and the wealthy who take no heed. Where is your compassionate God?

What about the atrocities, the murders, rapes, the wars in the name of religion, children molested, children learning how to steal and bash? What about the men, women and children blown to pieces just because someone wants something they are not getting? Where is your all-powerful God then?

If I was all-powerful, I would soon put an end to all this. I would deal with all who think to get their way by killing just anyone who happens to be around.

What about those who make killing look exciting? A manly thing to do? And the drug scene – the dope and the pedlars? Your all-seeing God seems to allow them to flourish and get rich beyond the imagination of ordinary folk.

The greatest obscenity of all is weapons of nuclear warfare, hoarded in their monstrous piles. What is the cost of these?

Where is your God? *Out There?*

To reply I would say that first of all you need to accept that there is a creator of the universe, that there is a mind behind this creation. I believe that the creator of the universe in which our planet dwells contains all personality, male and female. No way can this personality be divided into male and female as we are. It is a perfect whole because the substance of the creator/godhead is perfect love, energy, and power, which cannot be separated or activated other than as a whole.

The creator poured into our planet this love, energy and power and gave us the ability to respond or reject. Maybe a parable would help here. Parents have a son and daughter who, as they grow up, decide to leave home and go overseas. The parents give their consent and send them off with good wishes and a request for them always to keep in touch. But they go their ways; live their lives making their own decisions until they lose touch. Troubles come, but these children have lost the ability to call their parents and ask for help and advice. And they lose their way.

The parents grieve and suffer, but are powerless. They want and need the response and love of their children. But the link has been cut and it can only be restored by the son and daughter making contact.

No parable is perfect and neither is this one. The parents in the parable cannot contact their children; they have lost touch. God is always in touch with each one of us, but never uses force. Love cannot be forced; only given.

So… it would seem it is up to us. What a responsibility; what a challenge. We have within us the ability to absorb this great love, energy and power, to receive it and to respond to it. I wonder why we find this so hard to do? We know that life on this planet, on sea, land and in the air is dependent on us. There is an urgency here.

Will we learn and respond in time?

A Happening

Last evening I walked into my kitchen and saw a bee, quite still, on the outside of the window pane. It was so still I thought it must be dead. 'A funny place for a bee to die,' I said to myself, so I started to talk to it and stroke it through the glass to see if it would move.

After a time its antennae moved so I knew it was alive. 'A strange place to rest,' I thought, and so got on with preparing my dinner and forgot all about it.

This morning I went through to the kitchen and drew the curtains. As I reached for the jug I saw the bee in the same place as last evening and in the same posture. Then to my utter astonishment, I saw a baby bee, very close to its mother, yet not touching her as it moved quite rapidly up and down the window pane and around her. My eyes were glued to this amazing sight, while mother did not move except for her antennae, which were busy sending out messages.

After a time I said to myself, 'Come on, girl, you can't spend the whole day watching a baby bee and its mum,' so went on to make my morning cuppa.

When I looked back at the window pane, there was nothing there. No baby bee, no mum: it was as if I had dreamt it.

But I hadn't.

I couldn't forget what I had seen. I was like a dog with a bone as I moithered over the happening. (Lovely word, moither: pensive, persistent thought.) I remembered the activity of the baby bee. So very busy as it scuttled around, enjoying its freedom. Yet the freedom seemed to be contained within the orbit of Mum's antennae control, so it could receive messages of guidance and loving care.

I thought, 'There is quite a bit of me there. My life has been busy and free and yet contained within the orbit of God's antennae control, so that I have been able to receive messages of guidance and loving care.' Of course there is a difference. Mother bee's antennae are concerned with her baby bee, whereas God's antennae are full of energy, power and loving care, which are poured out and into everything and everyone.

We call it life.

But I have discovered, along with countless others, that this energy can be personalised by our response and by keeping close within the orbit of the love of God. So we are helped through life even in the tiny, daily happenings. What we miss when we think we can cope on our own!

Clever baby bee to be so wise.

Trees

As I stood in the forest and looked up at the canopy spread above me I found myself comparing it with the world and the people who live therein.

Daily I listen to the world news and every day I hear of war and horrors unspeakable. Nations fighting nations; people hurting people, by murder, rape, theft; and people without hope committing suicide.

As I stood in the peace and stillness of the forest my mind cried out, 'Why, oh why, cannot the peoples of the world live together like the trees above me?'

Trees in a forest live side by side in close proximity, their roots and their branches meeting and intertwining; the oak and the wattle are so different, yet they share the same space. There is no territorial fighting here. The oak does not say to the wattle, 'This is my piece of land, you cannot have it or share it.'

Yet the oak and the wattle have antecedents that go back in history, as do the people of the world.

The trees grow up side by side, sharing the nourishment from the soil, the rain and the sun. As they grow bigger and older their branches overlap, forming a canopy of protection for all the smaller life on the forest floor. These small plants have a right to space – to live out their cycle of living – and they are given their space.

The forest is not perfect. Plants and trees do die. Some feed and live off the life of others. Even so, what lessons are here for us to learn. We should stand, look up, listen and learn.

❧

Reality: A Wider Dimension

Sometimes we forget how very small we are and how very limited is our knowledge, our experience, our sensitivity.

Because we forget these things we tend to think we know all there is to know, that our experience of life is the whole of life, that our sensitivity has picked up all the waves of light colour, sound and thought.

Because we cannot see a thing or a dimension we say it is not there. Because we cannot prove a thing, or a greater life, we say it does not exist.

By what right do we claim such omniscience?

If a limpet clinging to a rock in a pool could think and clarify its thoughts, wouldn't it say much the same thing? That the whole of life existed in the pool in which it lived?

Imagine two people standing on the edge of a rock pool admiring the beauty of colour and the variety of life to be seen as they watch. But the limpet in the pool would be quite unaware of the two people above. It would be unable to see them or to comprehend the life they live. The greatness of the world they take for granted would be beyond its grasp. The speed with which they could move on earth or in the sky would boggle its mind. The language they spoke, the air they breathed, everything about them would be so colossal, so real, so magnificent that it would be too much to bear. So the limpet is spared; its eyes are 'holden.' So far and no further can its understanding go.

Today people tend to say that God and heaven are not 'out there' because astronauts have been 'out there' and they did not see either God or heaven.

Maybe we have more in common with the limpet than we like to think?

APPENDIX TWO

Newspaper Cuttings

'It Was Like A Miracle' *The Press*, **Christchurch, 14 March 1998**
The Rev. Glenys Lewis has, in her quiet way, been at the forefront of changes for women in the Anglican Church since she arrived in Christchurch in 1960.

Making a noise has not been the style for this tall, imposing woman, who was awarded a CBE 30 years after her appointment by the Anglican Council of Women to start a movement which led to the first women priests being appointed in 1978.

She trained as a nurse in Britain, became a lay worker for the church, and then was head deaconess in Guildford, England. In 1960 Deaconess Lewis came here as the first woman hospital chaplain at Christchurch Hospital.

'It was clear at that time that few women were coming forward for ordination in the deaconate. Only two dioceses had deaconesses at that time,' she says.

Miss Lewis was appointed to travel throughout New Zealand to drum up support for a deaconess training house. She did so, alone, and by car. She was supported by the seven bishops. It was not an easy task in many ways, but Miss Lewis, 86, plays down the opposition at the time.

She spoke to thousands up and down the country about ordination to the permanent deaconate for women and, in 1966, a house opened in Auckland with Miss Lewis as head deaconess. Theological training was taken at St John's College and she well remembers the day, six years before, when she was on her travels. The warden told her that she was the first woman to sit at high table for dinner.

Three years later deaconess students were allowed to train and live at St

John's and, as Miss Lewis puts it: 'It was like a miracle. Suddenly the whole caboose was wide open. It was staggering.'

From about this time the ordination of women to the priesthood became an issue in New Zealand, and was dealt with by the diocesan synods and General Synod. It was finally agreed in 1976, with the exception of the Wellington Synod. Wellington's appeal was not successful in the next year.

Her Auckland training home closed and Miss Lewis retired to Christchurch. In 1978 she was asked by the bishop to let her name go forward for ordination. 'At first I turned it down as I thought I had finished my ministry.'

That was not to be. Three Auckland women were ordained as priests first – making history in the worldwide Anglican community, and on February 19, in Christchurch, six women were ordained: Olive Ault and Jean Henderson were followed by Carole Graham and Margaret Wood on February 24, and Glenys Lewis and Melva Finney on February 26. Today about 35 women are ordained as priests.

Once ordained Miss Lewis went back to work, first as a hospital chaplain, and then temporary vicar of St Anne's, St Martins, followed by relieving work at St Saviour's, Sydenham and Oamaru. 'In 1978 we all felt a sense of fulfilment. The male clergy supported us magnificently.'

'Too Few Women Leaders', by Jo Myers, *Manawatu Evening Standard,*
1 November 1993

With the increasing numbers of women being ordained in the Anglican
Church, it's surprising more are not taking on leadership roles in the church,
says the woman who was in charge of the first women's Anglican theological
college in the country.

Reverend Glenys Lewis, 82, who visited Palmerston North last week, was
invested at Government House on Thursday with the CBE she was awarded
in the Queen's Birthday Honours list.

Miss Lewis was given the CBE for her services to the Anglican Church.
The citation says she is regarded as a pioneer in both England and New
Zealand, promoting the ordination of women.

She came to New Zealand in 1960 to work as a hospital chaplain and three
years later was asked by the Bishop of Christchurch to travel around New
Zealand telling people about the ministry of women in the church.

'I spoke to women's groups, preached in cathedrals and talked to synods
about the role of women in the church. I was the only woman who'd been
allowed to sit at the high table in the refectory at St John's Theological College
in Auckland [where men were trained for the ministry].'

By 1966 the first training school for women ministers was set up in Auckland and Miss Lewis was appointed head deaconess and warden. Four years
later Deaconess House was closed and women were accepted at St John's
College.

'That speaks volumes for the progress we made, and for the way the men
accepted women in the ministry,' she said.

Today 50 per cent of the students at St John's are women.

'But you would have thought with the progress that's been made, there
would be more women in leadership roles in the church. There's only one
woman bishop and a couple of archdeacons.

'We've yet to arrive at total acceptance.'

The Form and Manner of Making of Deaconesses

'Warrawee',
Diamond Harbour,
Christchurch

16th March 1964

The Most Reverend the Archbishop of New Zealand
Bishop's Court
Napier

My dear Archbishop,
On the two occasions that we have met you have shown such kindness towards the work in which I am engaged that I venture to write to you on a matter that is very much in my mind just now. I know that you will realise that I have no personal gain in this matter as I believe my ordination to be valid and satisfactory. It is for the future of the Order of Deaconesses in this country that I write this to you, and because the deaconesses have not been approached, and therefore they are concerned to safeguard what seems to be important.

I understand that the Commission to consider authorising a Form of Service for 'The Form and Manner of Making of Deaconesses' will be presenting its findings, to General Synod next month, in the form of a Statue and a proposed Form and Manner of Making of Deaconesses. Also, I understand that once these are passed by General Synod any statement made by the Church in

England about Deaconesses will no longer be relevant to the Church of this Province. Therefore, it seems to me this is the time for making sure that the 'esse' of the Order is retained in the proposed Statute and 'Form and Manner of Making of Deaconesses'.

Briefly, the 'esse' is to be found in:-

i. the following statement which was contained in Resolutions passed by the Houses of Canterbury and York in 1939-41…

    'that the Order of Deaconesses is the one existing ordained ministry for women, in the sense of being the only Order of Ministry in the Anglican Communion to which women are admitted by episcopal imposition of hands'.

ii. in the first two rubrics of the English 'Form and Manner of Making of Deaconesses, where the word 'ordained' is twice used, as it is in the Ordering of Deacons.

It seems to me that in the Statute or the 'Form and Manner of Making of Deaconesses', or in both, the specific use of the term 'ordained' or 'ordered' should be used. Otherwise the whole character of the Order will be changed and there will be a confusion which will retard the growth of the Order in this country.

Please forgive me writing to you at a time when you must be so very busy.

Yours very sincerely,
Glenys Lewis
Deaconess

**The Form and Manner of Making of Deaconesses
adopted by Upper House of Canterbury and York**

Before he *ordains* a woman as Deaconess, the Bishop shall by careful enquiry
satisfy himself as to her character, her training and her general fitness: he
shall by examination ascertain that she has adequate knowledge of the Bible,
of the creeds and the doctrine of the Church, of the history of the Church
and of the Book of Common Prayer: and he also shall require her to make
and sign a declaration that she believes the doctrine of the Church of England
as set forth in the book of Common Prayer to be agreeable to the Word of
God and that she will at all times teach in accordance with the same.

When the day appointed by the Bishop (which shall be a Sunday or Holy-
day) is come, the Archdeacon or some other priest (approved by the Bishop)
shall present unto the Bishop (sitting in his chair near the holy table) the
woman who desires to be *ordained* Deaconess (suitably habited), saying these
words:

Reverend Father in God…

The Bishop: Take heed that the person…

The Archdeacon shall answer: I have enquired of her…

Then the Bishop shall say to the people:
Brethren, if there be any of you who knoweth any grave cause by reason of
which this woman ought not to be admitted to the office of Deaconess, let
him come forth and shew what that impediment is.

And if any grave cause be objected, the Bishop shall cease from ordering the
woman until such time as he is satisfied that there is no impediment.

Then the Bishop shall commend the woman now found meet to be *ordered*
to the prayers of the congregation: for the which prayers there shall be silence
kept for a space.

Then shall be sung or said the service for the communion as followeth:

Collect

Epistle

Then, after the Epistle, the Bishop shall examine her who is to be *ordered*, standing before him in the presence of the people, after this manner.

Do you trust that you are…

Answer: I trust so…

The Bishop: Do you believe the Christian Faith…

Answer: I do believe it.

The Bishop: It appertaineth to the office of a Deaconess in the place where she shall be appointed to serve, in things both temporal and spiritual; to minister to the welfare and happiness of those to whom she is sent; to give instruction in the Holy Scriptures and in the Christian Faith, and to help the Minister of the parish in his work of preparing candidates for Baptism and Confirmation; to assist at the administration of Holy Baptism; to advise and pray with such women as desire help in difficulties and perplexities; to intimate the names of those who are in need, sickness, or other distress unto the Minister of the Parish…
Will you do this gladly and willingly?

Answer: I will…

Then, all kneeling, the Bishop, standing up and laying his hands upon the head of the woman humbly kneeling before him, shall say:
    Take thou authority to execute the office of a Deaconess in the Church of God committed unto Thee. In the Name of the Father and of the Son, and of the Holy Ghost. Amen.

Then shall the Bishop deliver to her the New Testament, saying; Be diligent to study the things that are written in this Book, that, as much as in thee lieth thou mayest teach the gospel of the grace of God and be an example of faith and holy living.

Then shall be read the Gospel.

**Proposed Form and Manner of Making of Deaconesses
for adoption by the General Synod of the N.Z. Church**

When the day appointed by the Bishop is come, the Archdeacon or some
other priest (approved by the Bishop) shall present unto the Bishop (sitting
in his chair near the holy table) the woman who desires to be made a Deaconess (suitably habited), saying these words:

Reverend Father in God…

The Bishop: Take heed that the person…

The Priest shall answer: I have enquired of her…

Then shall be sung or said the service for the communion as followeth:
Collect
Epistle

Then, after the Epistle, the Bishop shall examine her who is to be admitted,
standing before him in the presence of the people, after this manner.

Do you trust that you are…

Answer: I trust so…

The Bishop: Do you believe the Christian Faith…

Answer: I do believe it.

The Bishop: It appertains to the office of a Deaconess in the place where she
shall be appointed to serve, in things both temporal and spiritual, to read
both Morning and Evening Prayer and the Litany, except those portions
reserved to the Priest; to preach; to give instruction in the Faith; to Baptise
in Church; to assist in such pastoral duties as may be intrusted to her.

Will you do this gladly and willingly?

Answer: I will…

Then, all kneeling, the Bishop standing up and laying his hands upon the head of the woman humbly kneeling before him, shall say:
I admit you to the office of a Deaconess in the Church of God. In the Name of the Father and of the Son, and of the Holy Ghost. Amen.

Then shall be read the Gospel.